YOUR EYES:
AN OWNER'S MANUAL

JAMES F. COLLINS, M.D., F.A.C.S.

INFINITY PRESS OF LONG ISLAND, LTD.

PREFACE

This book was written to help you take better care of one of your most precious possessions—your sense of sight. Despite the proliferation of informational pamphlets, patient newsletters, and other educational materials devoted to vision care, a great deal of confusion and misinformation still abounds. It is hoped that this book will help to clarify things a bit.

YOUR EYES: An Owner's Manual was written from the viewpoint of the **ophthalmologist**, a medical doctor (M.D.) who has specialized in optical, medical, and surgical eye care. The training of an ophthalmologist includes four years of college (pre-medical), four years of medical school (M.D. Degree), a year of internship, and three years of residency in ophthalmology and ophthalmological surgery. An optional year or two may then be spent in subspecialty "fellowship" training. This rigorous and extensive background prepares the ophthalmologist to be a senior authority and expert on the management of a full spectrum of eye disorders.

Other eye care professionals include optometrists (O.D.) and opticians. The **optometrist** commonly treats optical disorders with glasses, contact lenses, and low vision aids, and examines for abnormalities of the eyes. There is considerable variation from state to state in the U.S. with regard to regulations governing the full scope of optometric care. State and local agencies can provide further information. The **optician** fabricates and dispenses eye wear (glasses and sometimes contact lenses).

The reader is advised to use this book as a reference and general guide to eye care and not as a manual for treatment. There is no substitute for proper professional eye care when problems arise. **Do not attempt to self-treat or to treat others except where absolutely necessary as outlined under emergency first aid care.**

ACKNOWLEDGMENTS

Grateful appreciation is expressed to the following individuals for their assistance in the production of this book:

Loretta C. Gross
Anita Marie Smith
Lia Argyropoulos
Debra A. Mulry, R.N.
Susan Carpenter, R.N.
Sharon Castellano, R.N.
Cathy Sidorski, R.N.
George Wollman, O.D.
William H. Luce, Optician
Thomas Guthlein, Optician
Gregory C. Persak, M.D.
Susan Margolis, M.D.

Special thanks for encouragement and support are extended to:

The Vistech Corporation

2nd Edition

CONTENTS

HOW TO USE THIS BOOK

YOUR EYES: An Owner's Manual is organized to allow for quick and easy access to the information you need and is not necessarily intended to be read from front to back in that order.

The major divisions of the book include **Structure and Function**, which explains how the eyes work; **Care and Maintenance**, which covers both routine care and specialized treatment; and an **Encyclopedia of Ocular Disorders**, which lists and describes over one hundred disorders of the visual system in alphabetical order. These three major sections are interrelated by numerous "cross-references", which will allow you to obtain further information and background material relating to a topic of interest. Each section also stands on its own and can be read for an overview, quick reference, or review. The side tabs in the right margin provide for quick access to any of the major sections, and a detailed **index** includes virtually all topics of interest.

For those who are seeking more information or resources for special services, an extensive **appendix** is provided for this purpose.

Take a moment now to leaf through the book and familiarize yourself with its contents.

YOUR EYES:
AN OWNER'S MANUAL

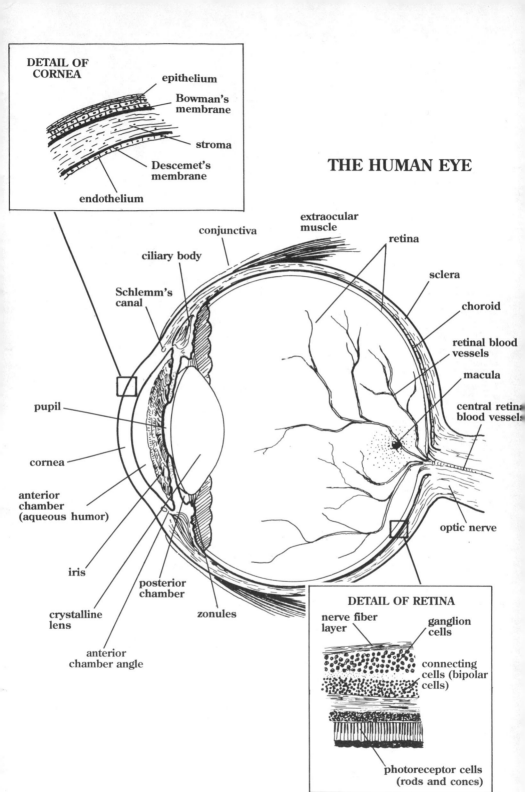

DETAIL OF CORNEA

epithelium

Bowman's membrane

stroma

Descemet's membrane

endothelium

THE HUMAN EYE

conjunctiva

extraocular muscle

retina

ciliary body

sclera

Schlemm's canal

choroid

retinal blood vessels

macula

central retina blood vessels

pupil

cornea

anterior chamber (aqueous humor)

iris

optic nerve

posterior chamber

crystalline lens

zonules

anterior chamber angle

DETAIL OF RETINA

nerve fiber layer

ganglion cells

connecting cells (bipolar cells)

photoreceptor cells (rods and cones)

STRUCTURE AND FUNCTION OF YOUR EYES

The human visual system is vastly complex and incredibly efficient. No man-made or computer-assisted creation even comes close to the marvelous function of the human eye.

In the following section, the anatomy (structure) and physiology (function) of the human eye and associated systems is discussed and depicted.

ANATOMY (STRUCTURE) OF THE EYE AND VISUAL SYSTEM

The eyeball, on average, is just under an inch in diameter (23-24 millimeters) and weighs approximately one quarter ounce (7.5 grams). The various parts of the eye are the:

sclera

the "white of the eye", a tough protective coat consisting of collagen and elastic tissues. The outermost layer of the sclera, called the episclera is a thin filmy substance with numerous blood vessels. Scleral thickness varies at different points ranging from the thinnest portion (0.3 millimeter) near the muscle insertions to the thickest (1.0-1.3 millimeters) at the back of the eye.

conjunctiva

the "skin" of the eye, a thin, filmy, transparent membrane covering the sclera. The conjunctiva also lines the inner side of the eyelids and contains numerous blood vessels and some mucus and tear glands.

cornea

the clear, transparent "window" of the eye. The cornea is approximately 12 millimeters in diameter and varies from a little more than one half millimeter in thickness centrally to a little more than a millimeter at the edges. The cornea consists of five distinct layers (from front to back): epithelium, Bowman's mem-

3

brane, stroma, Descemet's membrane and endothelium. The cornea contains numerous tiny nerve fibers, but no blood vessels.

anterior chamber

the space behind the cornea and in front of the iris and lens containing the bulk of the aqueous humor.

iris

the "colored part of the eye" (blue, brown, green, hazel, etc.). The iris contains two major sets of muscles (for dilating and constricting the pupil) and numerous blood vessels and pigment cells and granules.

anterior chamber angle

the part of the inner eye bounded by the cornea in front and the iris behind—contains part of the ciliary body (see below) and the aqueous drainage channels.

pupil

the black "hole" or "space" in the center of the iris—not actually a structure or component of the eye but an empty space much like the hole in a donut.

posterior chamber

the space behind the iris and in front of the vitreous humor— contains aqueous humor and the crystalline lens—also is the site for most current intraocular lens implantations after cataract surgery.

ciliary body

along with the iris and the choroid (see below) is considered part of the uveal tract or uvea of the eye. The ciliary body contains numerous blood vessels and various muscles for focusing the eye as well as the pigment cells and granules found in other parts of the uvea. The ciliary body also serves as the point of attachment for the zonules or suspensory ligaments of the lens and contains the cells which secrete the aqueous humor.

crystalline lens

along with the cornea, provides for the focusing of light rays entering the eye. The lens, consisting of regularly oriented protein fibers surrounded by a clear capsule, is a biconvex disc suspended in place by the zonules connecting it to the ciliary body. The curvature of the lens can change, providing variable focus power to the eye. In youth, the lens is "crystal clear" but gradually becomes somewhat yellowish and hazy with age *(see Cataract, page 132)*.

vitreous humor

the gel-like fluid which occupies the large space bounded by the lens and ciliary body in front and the retina and optic nerve in the back of the eye. The vitreous serves a cushioning and protective function for the eye and is normally optically clear. The vitreous consists of collagen, mucopolysaccharides and hyaluronic acid in a delicate balance. With time, the vitreous tends to contract and liquify and to separate from the retina. Condensed fibers and particles in the vitreous account for the "floaters" commonly seen by many people.

retina

the nerve cell layer of the eye which functions much like the film in a camera. The rest of the eye serves to focus light on to the retina where photochemical reactions occur as part of the process of vision. The retina is a thin, transparent tissue containing some 120 million separate rod cells (night vision) and 7 million cone cells

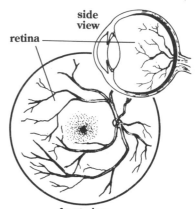

(day and color vision) as well as millions of other structural supporting and interconnecting cells. The *macula* is the sensitive, central, part of the retina which provides for sharp, detailed vision and contains the highest concentration of color-sensitive cone cells. The *fovea* is the center of the macula.

The retinal blood vessels course through the retinal substance and, along with the underlying choroid, supply the necessary nutrients and oxygen for normal retinal function. These blood vessels are remote branches of the large carotid arteries in the neck and can become occluded by fragments of calcium and cholesterol which chip off from partially blocked carotid arteries and flow into the eye *(see page 126)*.

choroid

the richly vascular, pigmented tissue situated between the retina and the sclera.

optic nerve

is the main "trunk line", consisting of a million or so separate nerve fibers, conducting nervous impulses from the retina to the brain. The optic nerve exits at the back of the eyeball and joins with the optic nerve of the fellow eye at the optic chiasm.

Other structures associated with the eyes and the visual pathways include the optic chiasm, optic tracts, geniculate bodies, optic radiations and visual cortex of the brain (see page 11).

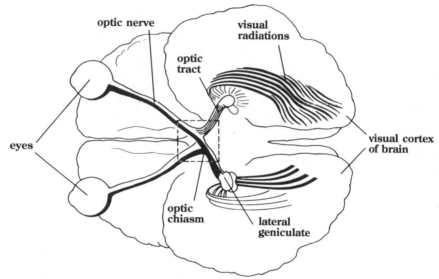

Brain with visual pathways (from below)

orbit

or "socket" of the eye is a roughly cone-shaped hollow in the skull formed by multiple bony plates. It contains the eyeball and optic nerve, lacrimal (tear) gland, extraocular muscles, orbital fat and a multitude of blood vessels and nerves which serve various functions of the eye. The orbits are also closely situated to the sinus cavities.

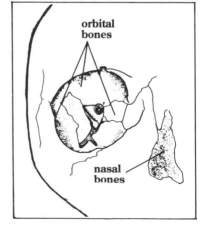

extraocular muscles

are tiny extremely sensitive muscles which move the eyeball in various directions. There are six muscles for each eye. The four rectus muscles arise at the apex or tip of the orbit and insert into the sclera five to seven millimeters behind the cornea. The superior oblique muscle arises from the apex of the orbit, passes

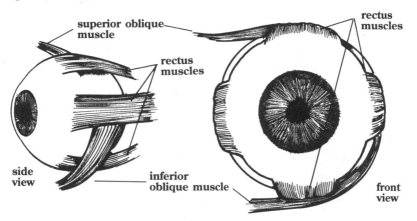

superior oblique muscle

rectus muscles

rectus muscles

side view

inferior oblique muscle

front view

forward through a small "pulley" called the trochlea near the front of the orbit and then passes back again to insert on the back side of the sclera. The inferior oblique muscle, unlike the other extraocular muscles, arises from the front part of the orbit and courses backward to insert on the back side of the sclera below the superior oblique muscle. Each muscle is operated by specialized nerve fibers and supplied with nutrients by tiny blood vessels. The third cranial nerve (oculomotor nerve) operates the inferior, medial and superior rectus muscles and the inferior oblique muscle as well as the levator (lifting) muscle of the upper lid and the pupillary and ciliary muscles. The fourth cranial nerve (trochlear nerve) operates the superior oblique muscle and the sixth cranial nerve operates the lateral rectus muscle.

eyelids

provide protection for the eyes and contain numerous glands and blood vessels. Beneath the skin of the lids is a muscle (orbicularis oculi) which, when contracted, closes the lids together. Beneath

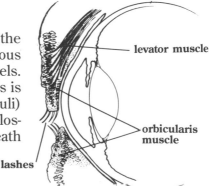

levator muscle

orbicularis muscle

lashes

7

the orbicularis muscle is the tarsus, the firm supporting element of the lid. The innermost layer of the lid is the palpebral conjunctiva, the smooth mucous membrane which makes contact with the eyeball. The upper lid is raised by contraction of the levator muscle.

lacrimal system *(tear system)* consists of the lacrimal glands (main gland behind the upper lid and accessory glands within the lids) which produce tear fluid. The tears, consisting of three components (watery, mucous and oily), course across the eyes providing lubrication and nutrients and form a small layer which rests on the lower lid (the tear meniscus). The tears then flow into the lacrimal lake at the inner corner of the eye and drain into the tear puncta, tiny openings in the upper and lower lids near the nose. The puncta, in turn, drain the tears into the canaliculi, lacrimal sacs and tear ducts which enter into the back of the nose. The connection between the tear ducts and the nose is sometimes not established at birth leading to congenitally blocked tear ducts *(see page 131).*

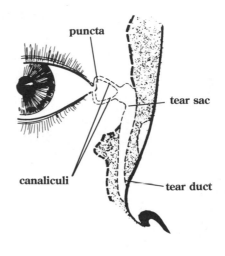

8

PHYSIOLOGY (FUNCTION) OF THE EYE AND VISUAL SYSTEM

"Physiology" refers to the "workings" of a biologic system. In this section we will cover the basics of how the eyes and the rest of the visual system function.

The Process of Seeing

The easiest way to understand the visual system is to follow some rays of light from where they first impinge on the eye to where they finally register as "vision" in the brain. Reference should be made to the drawings below and to the drawings and descriptions in the Anatomy section to better understand the sequence of events involved in the perception of vision.

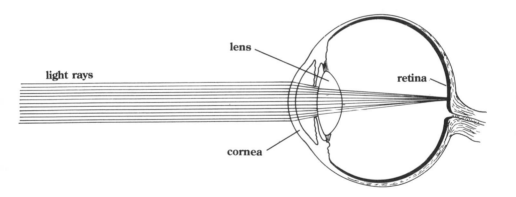

Light first passes into the eye through the transparent cornea which begins the process of focusing by bending (refracting) the light rays.

After crossing the anterior chamber, the light next passes through the pupil which automatically dilates (expands) or constricts (narrows) depending on the amount of light entering the eye. In dim light the pupil dilates to allow as much light as possible to enter the eye and in bright light the pupil constricts to prevent excessive light from entering the eye. The pupillary response to light is regulated by a complex neurologic reflex system and provides valuable diagnostic information regarding various ocular and neurologic disorders.

Just behind the pupil is the crystalline lens which further focuses the light, refining it into narrower beams that will provide clearer images. The lens, like the pupil, is also capable of variable function. Light rays arising from objects close to the eye require more focusing than light rays coming from distant objects. The lens automatically swells, increasing its curvature, to focus light from close range. This process of swelling is called *accommodation* and is produced by contraction of the ciliary body muscles. The ability of the lens to accommodate decreases progressively throughout life and eventually leads to the need for "close-range" or "reading" glasses *(see Presbyopia, pages 57 and 186)*. The act of accommodation is closely associated with two other reflexes relating to close-range vision, namely, pupillary constriction (different mechanism from the pupillary light response mentioned above) and convergence (inward turning of both eyes, *see Binocular Vision, page 12*). Together, accommodation, convergence and pupillary constriction are referred to as the "synkinetic near response".

After focusing by the lens, light then travels through the transparent vitreous humor and impinges on the retina.

The retina is a thin film of incredibly complex tissue lining the inside of the eyeball from the ciliary body on backwards. The retina contains hundreds of millions of specialized nerve cells arranged in complex patterns.The receptor cells ("vision receivers") are of two types, namely, rods and cones. The rods, which far outnumber the cones, function best under conditions of low illumination and reach maximal effectiveness after approximately thirty minutes in the dark. This explains why it takes time for vision to improve when walking into a darkened room such as a movie theater. There are approximately 120 million rod cells in each retina. The cones work best under conditions of bright illumination and also provide for detailed vision and color vision. The heaviest concentration of cone cells in the retina is in the macula or center of the retina. An even more specialized part of the macula, called the fovea is exclusively populated by extremely sensitive cone cells. The foveas are responsible for discerning fine detail such as reading, sewing, etc. The cone cells contain various pigments which are responsible for color vision. Absence of one or more cone pigments results in various color vision deficiencies *(see page 46)*.

Besides the rods and cones, many other types of connecting and supporting cells exist in the retina. Underlying the retina is the retinal pigment epithelium (RPE) which absorbs excess light and provides a nutritive function for the retina.

The electrical impulses that are generated by the interaction of light with the retinal receptor cells are transmitted through the other types of retinal cells to the optic nerve.

The optic nerve is a large trunk consisting of myriad smaller fibers. The optic nerves from each eye exit the eyeball in back and join each other at the base of the brain at a point called the optic chiasm.

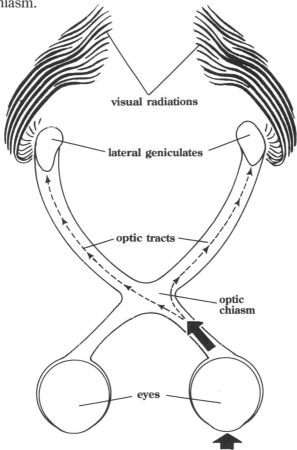

visual radiations

lateral geniculates

optic tracts

optic chiasm

eyes

In the optic chiasm a complex crossing of nerve fibers occurs and the visual impulses are then passed to the optic tracts which end in the lateral geniculate bodies. From here, visual impulses pass along the optic radiations which terminate in the occipital cortex at the back of the brain. In this area, there are extremely complex interconnections and visual association areas. It is at this point in the process where vision, as we know it, is perceived.

Binocular Vision and Ocular Motility

Binocular vision refers to the simultaneous function of both eyes in the creation of a single perceived image. This is accomplished by complex neurologic reflexes involving the afferent system (retina to brain) and the efferent system (brain to extraocular muscles). Under normal circumstances, the eyes are kept in parallel alignment in all directions of gaze and the simultaneously perceived images from both eyes are summated by the brain to a three dimensional "picture". The appreciation of three dimensions or depth perception is also referred to as *stereopsis*. When the eyes are misaligned for any reason (e.g., strokes, injuries, strabismus, etc.), binocular vision and stereopsis may be compromised or absent.

The extraocular muscles work in concert to keep the eyes aligned. Neurologic interconnections between muscle pairs ensure smooth, coordinated eye movements. When, for example, one wishes to look to the right, the lateral rectus muscle of the right eye and the medial rectus muscle of the left eye both contract an equal amount while the muscles on the opposite side of each eye relax. Ordinarily, all twelve eye muscles are constantly contracting and relaxing in the process of "everyday seeing" while, behind the scenes, an unimaginably complex neurologic feedback system is functioning without the individual's slightest awareness.

**co-contraction of muscles to
move the eyes in unison**

When the eyes become misaligned in young children, suppression (ignoring) of the image from the deviating eye occurs and amblyopia *(see page 126)* may develop. In an adult, sudden misalignment of the eyes from a stroke or an injury results in double vision or diplopia *(see page 146)*. Some individuals have intermittent double vision which can occur at times of fatigue, illness or inattention.

Other Specialized Functions

corneal clarity

The cornea, as described above, consists of multiple separate layers of cells. A specialized layer of cells called the endothelium lines the back surface of the cornea and is responsible for maintaining the clarity (transparency) of the cornea. The endothelial cells actually pump fluid out of the cornea overcoming the tendency of the cornea to swell and become cloudy or opaque like the adjacent white sclera. If a large enough number of endothelial cells are damaged by injuries, surgical procedures or corneal endothelial dystrophy *(see page 140)* the cornea will eventually swell and lose its transparency (corneal edema). Depending on the degree of swelling, this may become painful as well as visually disabling. In some cases the corneal edema is temporary and reversible; in others, a corneal transplant operation may be necessitated.

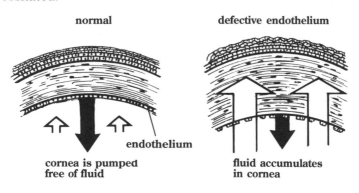

normal   defective endothelium

endothelium

cornea is pumped   fluid accumulates
free of fluid   in cornea

intraocular pressure

The anterior and posterior chambers of the eye are filled with aqueous humor which is produced by the ciliary body and circulates between the iris and the crystalline lens, through the pupil and into the anterior chamber. The aqueous is then drained from the eye through the trabecular meshwork which is situated in the anterior chamber angle. From here the aque-

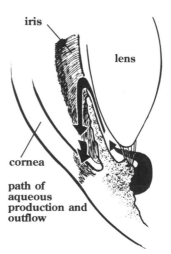

iris

lens

cornea

path of aqueous production and outflow

ous filters into various channels and eventually into the draining veins near the surface of the eye.

Ordinarily, there is a fine balance between the amount of aqueous being produced and the amount being filtered from the eye such that the intraocular pressure remains relatively constant and within tolerable limits.

If there is any obstruction to outflow of fluid from the eye at any point along the way, however, pressure can build up within the eye and glaucoma may develop *(see page 163). Note: many individuals tend to have "high normal" intraocular pressures but do not, in fact, have glaucoma.*

Intraocular pressure normally varies somewhat during the day and is subject to influence by many factors, including, general body fluid load, pressure within the draining veins, etc. The intraocular pressure can also be affected by different types of medication both intentionally and by side effect.

blood circulation of the eye

The eye, like all other organs in the body, requires the oxygen and nutrients provided by blood. Blood flows into the eye via the arterial system, passes to most of the ocular tissues through the capillary beds, and empties from the eye via the veins.

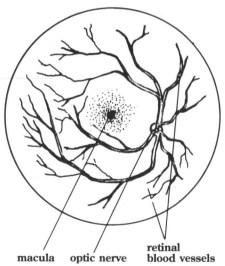

The retina has a particularly well developed system of arterioles (branches of arteries) capillaries and veins. The central retinal artery and its branches supply most of the retina and the central retinal vein drains the blood back out of the eye from all its branches and tributaries.

Any process which limits the flow of blood to the retina (clots, emboli, diabetic vascular damage, severe drop in systemic blood pressure, etc.) can result in damage to all or part of the retina with consequent loss of some visual function. The presence of emboli (mobile particles of calcium, cholesterol, etc. in the retinal arterioles is often an indicator of a circulatory problem further downstream (carotid

macula   optic nerve   retinal blood vessels

arteries in neck, heart valves, etc.) and may be an early warning sign of an impending stroke *(see retinal artery occlusions, page 190)*.

Insufficient drainage of blood through the retinal veins can also lead to serious visual problems due to blood spilling out into the retina and damaging its delicate neural structure. *(see retinal vein occlusions, page 194)*.

The choroid contains a vast network of blood vessels and capillaries which supply the outer segments of the retina. Damage to the choroid from sclerosis (hardening of the vessels) or injuries (choroidal rupture). etc. can also lead to serious visual consequences.

CARE AND MAINTENANCE OF YOUR EYES

Your eyes are a marvel of design, function and self-regulation. Most people think of their eyes as extremely delicate organs subject to damage at the slightest provocation. In actuality, the eyes are remarkably tough and resilient, made to last out a lifetime of continual use.

You must, however, do your part to help care for and maintain your sight. Modern ophthalmology uses incredibly advanced technology to diagnose and treat eye disorders but early detection of problems is critical to achieving good results in most cases. Equally important is the common sense avoidance of activities or situations which might endanger the health of your eyes. The following information should help you sort out what may and may not be important in the care and maintenance of your eyes. As always, when you are in doubt about a particular question CALL YOUR OPHTHALMOLOGIST for help.

Also included in this section is a summary of various eye examination procedures to help you better understand what your ophthalmologist is doing to help care for and maintain your sight.

GENERAL MEASURES

SOME "DO'S AND DON'TS" FOR YOUR EYES

DO:

- wear appropriate protective eye wear (e.g., wrap-around goggles when using tools that may jeopardize the eyes—especially power tools; proper shielding when exposed to radiant energy such as arc welding; protective goggles when exposed to chemicals, etc.).

- carefully check all labels, expiration dates and directions on any substance you are instilling in your eyes—many chemical eye injuries result from the mistaken use of various chemicals and medications not intended for the eyes—containers should be labeled "ophthalmic" preparation or have some other appropriate designation for use in the eyes.

- immediately and copiously flush your eyes with cold tap water (or other solution intended for the purpose) in the event of chemical contact with the eyes.

- learn the proper use of glasses, contact lenses and medications for your eyes and abide by them.

- occasionally check your own vision by covering one eye and then the other (with your glasses or contact lenses on, if appropriate) while looking at a sign or other detailed target—any significant changes should be reported to your ophthalmologist.

• rest your eyes periodically if doing prolonged close work (e.g., reading, sewing, computer work, etc.). Closing and relaxing the eyes as well as shifting focus to a distant object or getting up to walk about all help to relieve the ocular muscle stresses that lead to fatigue and eyestrain.

• use "hypoallergenic" or "allergy tested" eye make-up products and apply them carefully and sparingly.

• get your eyes examined periodically by your ophthalmologist *(see recommendations for routine care on page 25)*.

DON'T:

• don't ignore persistent symptoms such as blurred vision, pain, redness, etc. *(see important signs and symptoms, page 26)*.

• don't rub your eyes vigorously.

• don't overuse or "strain" your eyes—long hours reading or at the computer should be broken up by periods of rest.

• don't attempt to remove an ocular foreign body on yourself or another—serious damage can be done.

• don't stare at a dangerous source of radiant energy such as the sun during an eclipse, a blast furnace, arc welding torch, laser, sunlamp, etc.

- don't attempt to remove a "stuck" contact lens on yourself or another that has resisted the usual attempts at removal *(see trouble shooting contact lens problems, page 68)*.

- don't overuse "over the counter" decongestant eye drops—persistent irritation or redness requiring their use should be reported to your ophthalmologist.

- don't overdo the use of eye make-up—various allergies and inflammations of the eyes and eyelids can result—be especially careful to avoid contact of the make-up with the inside of the eyelids or the eyes themselves.

- don't attempt to self diagnose or treat eye disorders—see your ophthalmologist.

SOME FACTS AND FALLACIES
ABOUT YOUR EYES

Is it true that sitting too close to the TV can ruin one's eyes?

No. You can certainly tire or "strain" the eyes so this is not recommended but no physical damage will result. Children, in particular, tend to sit close and can often do so comfortably due to their large accommodative or "focus" reserve.

Sitting close to a TV or holding a book very closely may, however, indicate the presence of nearsightedness. Call your ophthalmologist for further advice.

Incidentally, it is usually recommended to keep a light on in the room at night while watching TV to avoid the concentrated focal glare from the brightly illuminated screen.

Can constant work on a computer screen cause eye damage?

As with the TV, no real damage can occur either from the proximity to the screen or from any "radiation" given off but the eyes can certainly become tired and uncomfortable.

It is, of course, necessary to have the proper prescription glasses if they are indicated and sometimes a special coating or tint on the lenses helps to relieve eyestrain. Many computers can now be outfitted with special glare reduction screens. Furthermore, it is recommended that periodic short breaks be taken to allow for relaxation of the focusing muscles of the eyes.

Can reading in poor light ruin one's eyes?

Once again, fatigue, discomfort and "eyestrain" can result but the eyes will in no way be physically harmed. Comfortable, easy reading is best achieved with the steady soft white light from an incandescent bulb. The light should ideally be situated behind the shoulder to avoid direct or reflected glare. The recommended wattage varies with the distance from the light and the ambient room lighting.

CARE & MAINTENANCE

21

Is it true that once someone is started in glasses a dependence results and stronger glasses will soon be necessary?

No. The eyes do not normally become physically dependent on the glasses. If vision is significantly improved by glasses, the individual will ordinarily be inclined to wear the glasses regularly.

Nearsighted children often continue to progress in the early years needing fairly frequent updates in their glasses but this is usually due to the inherited nearsighted trait being expressed gradually during the growing years rather than to any physical effects from wearing the glasses.

Similarly, adults past age forty often need reading glasses which need to be increased in strength every few years. This results from the natural progression of presbyopia *(see page 186)* and not from having worn the glasses. Abstinence from the use of a required eyeglass prescription does not "save" the eyes or prevent the future need for glasses.

Is it true that someone with an "eye condition" such as glaucoma or macular degeneration should "save" their vision by limiting the amount of reading or sewing that they do?

No. The presence of any chronic eye condition does not require one to limit the use of the eyes except as directed specifically by your ophthalmologist. Obviously, immediately following an eye injury or major eye surgery there are some limitations that are usually imposed but most chronic eye conditions will in no way be aggravated by use of the eyes.

Is it normal for a newborn's eyes to "cross"?

No. Many infants are born with the appearance of crossed eyes *(see pseudostrabismus, page 187)* which usually improves spontaneously but truly crossed eyes *(see esotropia, page 154)* require the early attention of an ophthalmologist.

Can one's eyes be harmed by wearing an incorrect prescription?

No. The eyes will not actually be harmed but could become quite uncomfortable and strained. Driving or operating other dangerous machinery would, of course, not be advisable with the incorrect prescription.

Can the eyes be strengthened by exercises?

Convergence insufficiency *(see page 139)* and certain other eye muscle coordination problems can sometimes be improved by specially prescribed eye exercise programs. Claims that near-sightedness and other true refractive errors can be "cured" by exercises have not been substantiated.

Can vision be improved through diet and nutrition?

Intensive research is currently being conducted to determine the role of diet and nutrition in the prevention and treatment of various eye diseases.

At the present time no specific guidelines can be given.

Certainly, where a diet is grossly deficient in vitamin A, serious eye disease can result and is indeed a major problem in underdeveloped countries. Supplementing a normal diet with carrots and vitamins etc. will not improve visual function. Conditions such as macular degeneration may benefit from vitamin therapy.

If vision is lost can an artificial eye be implanted?

No. Crude prototypes of implanted minicameras are in development but do not provide anything resembling the quality of normal human vision. Damaged corneas can be transplanted and artificial intraocular lenses can be implanted in place of cataracts but transplantation of entire eyes or implantation of functioning artificial eyes is beyond today's technology.

My eyes tend to tear a lot. Is it true that this signifies an underlying problem with my eyes?

Some degree of tearing from eyestrain, fatigue, and irritation from the sun, chemicals, pollutants and allergens is essentially normal. When tearing is excessive or constant, especially when accompanied by discharge or redness, there is usually a problem requiring attention *(see epiphora, page 152)*.

My eyes are very light sensitive—does that mean there is some problem?

Not necessarily. Many people, especially those with light colored eyes, tend to be bothered by bright lights. This is a natural protective reaction of the eyes.

Bright, sunny days, particularly in the presence of broad expanses of snow, ice or water which reflect the light, tend to cause light sensitivity in most people.

There are some pathologic conditions of the eyes, however, which can cause intensified or abnormal light sensitivity *(see uveitis, page 204; keratitis, page 173; and exotropia, page 160)*.

I tend to get headaches frequently. Are these likely to be due to my eyes?

Only a thorough exam can tell for sure but eye problems are not actually a common cause of headaches. More commonly, stress or muscle tension headaches, sinus problems or migraine are likely to be the culprits.

Among the potential eye-related causes of headaches are: uncorrected or poorly corrected refractive errors such as farsightedness, astigmatism or presbyopia *(see page 57)*, uncontrolled or poorly controlled glaucoma with very high pressures *(see page 163)*, and significant eye muscle imbalances such as convergence insufficiency *(see page 139)* or exophoria *(see page 158)*.

My son is constantly squinting and blinking his eyes. What could be the problem?

Squinting can signify the presence of a refractive error such as nearsightedness or an eye muscle imbalance. Frequently, however, squinting and forcible blinking can be temporary habits or tics without any abnormality of the eyes. Only a thorough medical eye exam can sort this out.

DETECTION OF EYE DISEASE

SUGGESTED SCHEDULE OF EYE EXAMINATIONS

- eyes are normally examined shortly after birth by the pediatrician or neonatologist—an ophthalmologist is consulted as necessary.

- if no abnormalities are seen or suspected, a first routine examination of the eyes should be performed by an ophthalmologist at or around three years of age—at this age most children are able to cooperate for a reliable exam and to "read" the picture chart; if a problem such as amblyopia *(see page 126)* is discovered, it can usually be effectively treated at this age.

- preschool and school screening exams are usually carried out yearly in most areas from age four on.

- if no abnormalities have been noted up to this point and there is no other reason to suspect a problem (e.g., family history of eye disorders, etc.), another routine exam can be performed by the ophthalmologist at age six.

- the next routine exam should be at about age thirteen if there are no visual problems in the interim.

- students beginning college or graduate school should also undergo a routine eye exam as should those starting a job requiring intensive use of the eyes such as computer terminal operators, etc.

- after age forty, routine exams by an ophthalmologist should be performed at one or two year intervals mostly to screen for glaucoma; it is also at this age that reading vision generally diminishes *(see presbyopia, page 186)* requiring periodic reading glass or bifocal updates.

- after age sixty-five, yearly routine eye examinations are recommended since the incidence of glaucoma, cataracts and macular degeneration rise sharply at this age.

IMPORTANT SIGNS AND SYMPTOMS

The following are all important signs or symptoms that should prompt you to call your ophthalmologist or appropriate health care agency for assistance on an emergency basis *(see page 107)*.

- **Sudden loss of vision or sudden blurred vision** (one or both eyes, partial or complete, temporary or on-going, with or without pain).

- **Double vision** (i.e., seeing two images where there should only be one). This may be horizontal (side by side) or vertical (one image above or diagonal to the other) may also be intermittent or constant and can occur only with both eyes open (binocular double vision) or from only one eye (monocular double vision). **Sudden onset of double vision** requires emergency evaluation.

- **"Flashes"** or **"Flashes and Floaters"** (sparkling or flashing lights with or without dark moving spots).

- **Sudden marked distortion in vision** (metamorphopsia) (one or both eyes unrelieved by blinking or "refocusing" the eyes).

- **Severe redness of the eye** (one or both eyes, with or without pain, with or without discharge, with or without blurred vision).

- **Severe pain in the eye** (one or both eyes, may be sudden or gradually building in intensity, with or without loss of vision, with or without redness and/or discharge).

Obviously, any injury to the eyes should be reported to your ophthalmologist or other appropriate health care agency on an emergency basis. Many injuries may be trivial and not vision threatening but it is always safer to seek professional advice. Your ophthalmologist will often be able to determine from the nature of the injury and the attendant symptoms whether or not an immediate examination is warranted *(see page 108 for further information on accidents and injuries)*.

The following are signs or symptoms that should be reported to your ophthalmologist or other appropriate health care agency but not ordinarily on an emergency basis except as denoted otherwise:

- *Blurred vision* (one or both eyes)—if sudden in onset or steadily worsening, blurred vision should be reported immediately—if onset is gradual and symptom is mild, stable and unaccompanied by other signs or symptoms, blurred vision can usually be reported on a non-emergent basis.

- *Itching of eyes and/or lids*—if severe and associated with marked redness or swelling—should be reported immediately.

- *Dryness of the eyes.*

- *Tearing*—if severe and associated with significant redness pain, or loss of vision—should be reported immediately.

- *Burning of the eyes.*

- *Scratchy or foreign body sensation*—if severe or following any sort of eye injury—should be reported immediately.

- *Light sensitivity (photophobia)*—if severe or associated with pain or loss of vision, should be reported immediately.

- *Swollen or puffy eyelids*— if severe, associated with pain or following an injury—should be reported immediately.

- *Painful eye movements*—if associated with any loss of vision—should be reported immediately.

- *Tenderness of the eyes.*

- *"Haloes" around lights*—if rather sudden and associated with pain, redness and blurred vision—should be reported immediately.

- *"Floaters" (flies, specks, cobwebs, spots, etc.)*—if large or associated with "flashes" , "smoky" vision, or the appearance of a curtain, veil or shade being drawn over the vision—should be reported immediately.

- *Lid twitching (blepharospasm).*

- *Discharge*—if associated with significant redness, pain or or loss of vision—should be reported immediately.

- *"Night blindness"*

- *Protrusion of the eye(s) (proptosis, exophthalmos)*—if sudden or associated with pain or loss of vision—should be reported immediately.

- *Zig-zag" or "jagged" lines* in vision (with or without headache)—if persistent or in the elderly, should be reported immediately.

- *Fluctuating vision.*

- *Droopy lid(s).*

- *Unequal pupils*—if recent onset and pupils were previously known to be equal—should be reported immediately.

- *Discolorations of the eyes*—e.g., whites (sclera) appear blue, yellow, etc. or dark spots noted.

- *Headaches*—if occurring only with use of the eyes e.g., while reading, etc. report to ophthalmologist; if occurring under other circumstances, report to family practitioner, internist, pediatrician, etc.

- *Any other signs or symptoms* related to the eyes which seem out of the ordinary—when in doubt, call for assistance.

DIAGNOSTIC MODALITIES—
EVALUATING YOUR EYES

Following is a survey of various techniques and procedures that may be used by your ophthalmologist to evaluate the health and functional status of your eyes.

Many tests and measurements are now performed by highly trained technicians or nurses. Your ophthalmologist interprets the results and personally performs any tests requiring his or her special skills.

Prior to the performance of any tests or examinations, a thorough history is usually taken by the doctor or a trained technician or nurse and usually covers the "chief complaint" or reason for the current visit. Pertinent past medical history, a list of current medications and allergies , and past ocular history are also obtained. Any eyeglasses you may have are also usually checked at this time—the prescription can be read directly from your glasses by a special device called a lensmeter.

External Examination

External examination consists of a general inspection of the face, orbits, eyelids and eyes. Usually performed in normal room light with the aid of a flash light or "transilluminator", this very important part of the general examination often provides clues to underlying problems and direction for the remainder of the exam. Years of experience are required to properly evaluate the eyes by this means. Subtle drooping of a lid, slight protrusion of one eye or the presence of a small skin cancer on an eyelid could all escape detection and lead to serious consequences if not discovered.

Visual Acuity Testing

Visual acuity testing, the cornerstone of the eye examination, measures the potential of the eyes' central (straight ahead) vision.

Typically, a Snellen type chart (may be projected, wall hung etc.) like the one on the right is used and the smallest line that the subject can read is recorded for each eye. Testing is usu-

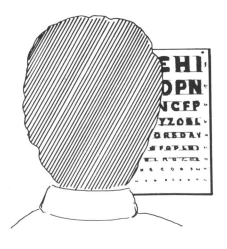

ally performed with and without glasses or contact lenses to determine the best corrected and uncorrected vision of the eyes. Numbers, "illiterate E's" (letter E's oriented in various directions), and special pictures are also used where appropriate.

Using the Snellen notation, a score written as a fraction, is given to each eye. 20/20 is considered ideal. This means the eye sees at a distance of twenty feet (or equivalent) what it should ideally see at twenty feet. When an eye sees at twenty feet what it ideally should be able to see from a distance of forty feet it is scored as 20/40. The higher the second number—the worse the vision. It is important to note that each eye is given a Snellen score so that, for example, one eye could be 20/20 and the other could be 20/60. (*Note: in countries where the metric system of measurement is in use, six meters replaces the twenty feet and ideal vision is 6/6*). A score of 20/15 is actually better than 20/20 and signifies that the individual sees at twenty feet what the normal eye must be at a distance of fifteen feet to see.

When visual acuity is below what can be measured on the chart at the standard distance, chart and subject can be moved closer together. A score of 5/200 would mean that the individual sees at five feet what he should be able to see at a distance of two hundred feet!

Contrast Sensitivity and Glare Testing

Conventional vision testing with the Snellen chart, as described above, employs high contrast black on white characters. Research has now shown that this means of testing only evaluates one aspect of vision; much more useful "real-life" information may be obtained with the use of contrast sensitivity testing which employs shades of gray in various patterns. Some individuals with 20/20 Snellen acuity may be compromised by early 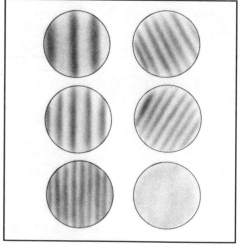 cataracts or glaucoma, etc. which may very significantly impair their ability to discriminate more subtle visual stimuli thus interfering with their ability to drive safely especially at night. These individuals may test very poorly with contrast sensitivity targets.

The use of contrast sensitivity in routine testing will become more and more common in the future as more data is accumulated and new standards for "normal vision" are set.

Glare testing is also becoming more widely used and accepted as a means of evaluating vision under conditions of glare (bright sun , reflections, oncoming headlights, etc.). Special testing devices which simulate glare conditions are being widely introduced. As with contrast sensitivity, many individuals with otherwise "good Snellen acuity" may be suffering significant visual impairment due to cataracts and corneal disorders, etc. that could only be detected by this special means.

Slit Lamp Examination

The slit lamp is one of the most important diagnostic tools used by the ophthalmologist. It is basically a binocular microscope which can project a narrow "slit-like" beam of light *onto* and *into* the eye. By this means, the ophthalmologist can visualize an "optical cross-section" of various parts of the eye under high magnification. A tremendous amount of important information about the health and optical status of the eye can be determined by this means.

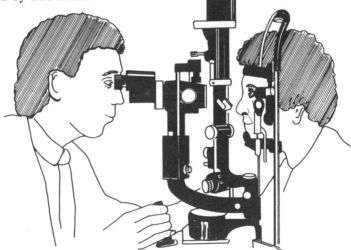

The slit lamp also serves as a delivery system for many types of ophthalmic lasers and accommodates various diagnostic attachments including the Goldmann applanation tonometer for measuring the pressure within the eye as part of glaucoma testing. Cameras can also be mounted on the slit lamp to allow for high powered documentary photographs of the eye.

Foreign body, suture and lash removal, etc. are also commonly performed with the aid of the slit lamp.

Refraction

Refraction is the process by which the refractive error (farsightedness, nearsightedness, astigmatism) of the eye is measured. This can be accomplished in various ways. In many offices a computerized device called an autorefractor is first used (usually by a technician) to obtain a close estimate of the refractive error. The autorefractor employs a very sensitive scanning device that "reads" the focusing characteristics of the eye and prints out the data for further evaluation. Some autorefractors go a step further to refine the readings to the point where a suggested final eye glass prescription is generated. More commonly, however, the readings are then set into a manual refractor or trial frame for further refinement by the technician, optometrist or ophthalmologist. This is the part of the refraction where the subject is asked which of two different lens choices seems better or clearer ("one or two," etc.).

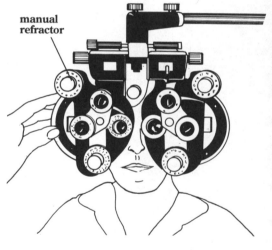

manual refractor

An alternative to the use of the autorefractor is retinoscopy performed by the technician, optometrist or ophthalmologist. By this means the eyes can be "scanned" directly by the operator. A streak or spot of light is projected by the hand held retinoscope onto the retina. An orange-colored reflection is seen through the pupil much like the orange/red pupillary reflection seen in many flash photographs. By moving the streak of light in various directions, a visual estimate of the degree of nearsightedness, farsightedness or astigmatism can be made and the appropriate lenses placed in front of the eye to neutralize the refractive error. The final lens power is then determined by refinement as described above.

In small children or individuals who can not reliably respond to the refinement questions, *cycloplegic* refraction can be used for very accurate measurements. This involves the use of eye drops which dilate the pupil and temporarily suspend the eye's ability to change focus. Retinoscopy can then be carefully performed to arrive at the final eye glass prescription. Cycloplegic refraction is also indicated in cases of strabismus *(see page 199)*.

Evaluation Of The Pupils

The pupils *(see pages 4 and 9)* normally dilate (open wider) in dim lighting and constrict (become smaller) in bright lighting. The pupils also normally constrict when the eye is focusing on an object at close range. In most people they are also equal or very close to equal in size.

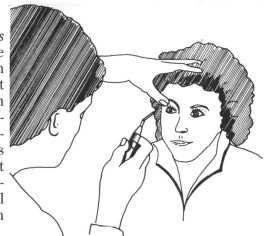

The ophthalmologist frequently checks that the pupils are indeed performing as described above. A small light source (penlight or transilluminator) is used to test the pupillary reactions. In addition to checking for equality in size and proper reactions to light there are a number of other subtle characteristics of the pupils that the ophthalmologist evaluates which can tell a great deal about the eyes and can provide clues to various underlying neurologic problems.

Keratometry

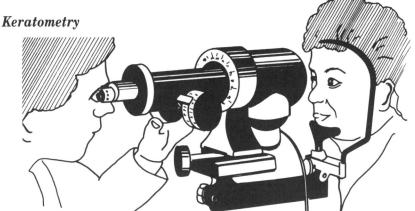

Keratometry is the measurement of the curvature of the cornea *(see page 3)*. The corneal curvature is a major determinant of the refractive error ("focusing status") of the eye and must be accurately measured for contact lens fitting and in the preoperative calculation of intraocular lens powers prior to cataract surgery. In addition, there are various other technical uses for keratometry.

Keratometry can be performed automatically by sophisticated scanning devices (autokeratometer) or manually.

Keratoscopy

In keratoscopy, a series of concentric rings of light is projected onto the cornea. Normally, the reflection of this ring pattern on the cornea should be very smooth, regular and symmetrical. In various disorders of the cornea the reflection is distorted. Observation (and photographing) of this distortion provides valuable information to the ophthalmologist about the underlying diagnosis and future course of the condition. Computerized **corneal topography** is a newer, more sophisticated procedure now gaining wide acceptance among ophthalmologists.

Pachymetry

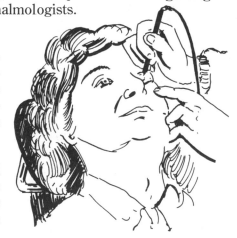

The thickness of the cornea can be measured by a device called a pachymeter. This information is useful in diagnosing and following the progress of edema (swelling) of the cornea.

Pachymetry is also critical in the performance of some refractive surgeries *(see page 90)* to gauge the proper depth of incisions in the cornea.

Gonioscopy

Gonioscopy is the procedure whereby the anterior chamber angle of the eye is visualized and evaluated. Ordinarily, this area of the eye can not be directly seen without the use of a special lens to bend or reflect light rays into this tiny recess.

The most commonly used goniolens has an angulated mirror mounted within a form fitting, hand held contact lens which is applied directly to the eye after instilling an anesthetic drop. The ophthalmologist can then look into this mirror with the aid of the slit lamp *(see page 31)* and clearly visualize a magnified view of the iris and anterior chamber angle.

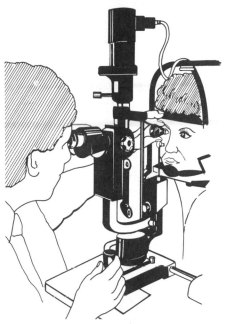

Gonioscopy is an invaluable aid in the diagnosis and classification of cases of glaucoma. The anterior chamber angle is the site of obstruction to outflow of fluid from the eye in glaucoma and must be carefully inspected to determine the exact nature of a particular case of glaucoma.

Gonioscopy is also useful prior to insertion of anterior chamber intraocular lens implants to ensure that there are no abnormalities that would complicate the operation.

Specially coated goniolenses are also used for certain laser operations for the treatment of glaucoma.

Ophthalmoscopy

Ophthalmoscopy (also called fundoscopy) refers to the visualization by the ophthalmologist of the interior of the eye by the use of an ophthalmoscope. The optic nerve, blood vessels, retina, choroid and part of the ciliary body can be seen by this means. Dilating drops enhance the ophthalmoscopic exam by enlarging the pupil.

The direct ophthalmoscope is a small hand held instrument containing a battery in the handle, a light source, an aperture for viewing the fundus (curved inside surface of the eye) and a rotatable wheel with multiple tiny lenses for focusing the image. This is usually positioned very close to both the examiner's and the subject's eyes and provides the examiner with a bright magnified direct view of the interior of the eye. Only the back (posterior) half of the fundus can be seen by this means. A view of the front or anterior part of the fundus can be achieved with a specialized diagnostic contact lenses or with the indirect ophthalmoscope.

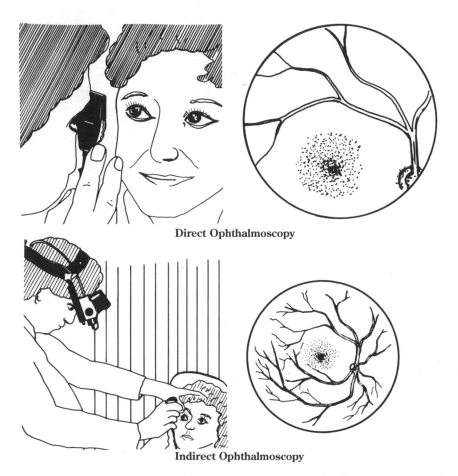

Direct Ophthalmoscopy

Indirect Ophthalmoscopy

The indirect ophthalmoscope uses a bright light source and binocular viewing system mounted on a head band worn by the examiner. A precision-ground hand held condensing lens is then held in front of the subject's eye and in line with the light source. A bright but inverted and only slightly magnified view of the interior of the eye is then obtained.

To view the extreme edges of the retina and the back part of the ciliary body by indirect ophthalmoscopy a small hand held *scleral depressor* is used to gently push these parts of the eye into view. This type of exam is used to inspect for a possible retinal tear at the edges of the retina.

Ophthalmoscopy can also be performed with various other lens systems including the slit lamp-mounted Hruby lens, the 90 diopter hand-held lens and various types of contact lenses also used with the slit lamp.

A tremendous amount of valuable information about the health and functional status of the eye can be learned through ophthalmoscopy. In addition, many generalized medical disorders can also be diagnosed by evaluating the appearance of the inside of the eye, particularly the blood vessels.

Endothelial Cell Photography and Counting

Endothelial cell photography (also called specular microscopy)is a specialized technique for imaging the "inner lining cells" of the cornea which are normally responsible for keeping the cornea clear and free of excess fluid. When these cells are either damaged or decreased in number the cornea may begin to swell and become cloudy. Certain eye injuries, inflammations and operations as well as some corneal dystrophies *(see page 140)* can cause endothelial cell damage.

Prior to some eye operations it may be very important to know the number and character of the endothelial cells since this information may influence the decision to operate or the choice of procedure.

By means of a very specialized photographic system this data can be obtained and compared to similar information obtained after surgery. The results of endothelial cell photography and counting can also be very helpful in the management of many corneal diseases.

Exophthalmometry

Exophthalmometry is the measurement of the protrusion of the eyes from the orbit ("socket"). Various conditions including some forms of thyroid disease, hemorrhages and tumors of the orbit, etc. can cause the eyes to protrude (called exophthalmos or proptosis). The amount of the protrusion and the difference between the two eyes can be measured quickly and easily with a number of different devices, the most popular being the Hertel exophthalmometer which uses a simple mirror system to gauge the degree of exophthalmos.

The measurements obtained are valuable for future comparison and in medical and surgical management decisions.

Ultrasonography

High frequency sound waves, beyond the range of human hearing, can be used to create "echo pictures" of the inside of the eye and orbit ("B-scans") as well as to obtain extremely accurate measurements of the eye (biometry using "A-scans") The technology involved is very similar to SONAR.

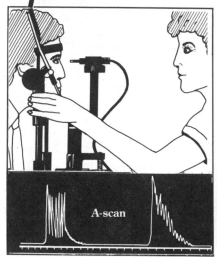 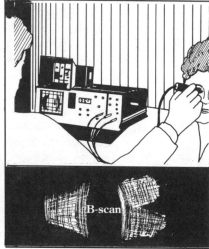

By this means the ophthalmologist can "see" inside an eye that is otherwise opaque to normal light due to corneal scars, cataracts, vitreous hemorrhages, etc.

Ultrasound is also used in the measurement of corneal thickness *(pachymetry, see page 34)* and for the generation of high frequency vibrations of a needle used in one form of cataract surgery (phacoemulsification).

Various other therapeutic uses of ultrasound (e.g., for the treatment of glaucoma) are being investigated.

Tonometry

Tonometry is the measurement of the pressure within the eye. This can be performed by the "air puff" device (noncontact tonometry) or by directly pressing on the anesthetized eye with a calibrated instrument, most commonly the applanation tonometer attached to the slit lamp *(see page 31)*.

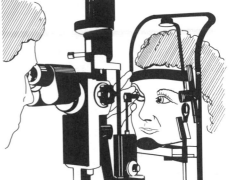

Tonometry is the cornerstone of glaucoma detection and treatment. Normal ranges for tonometry readings have been established by the measurement of thousands of individuals. Readings outside the normal range are then investigated for the possibility of glaucoma or other ocular disorders.

Tonography is a more involved procedure whereby the pressure in the eye is measured over a period of time yielding information about the "outflow facility" (ease of internal fluid drainage) of the eye.

In some cases where the diagnosis of glaucoma is uncertain, various provocative tests may be performed to see if the intraocular pressure can be significantly elevated. These tests are always performed in a very controlled and safe fashion under the supervision of the ophthalmologist. In cases of possible angle closure glaucoma, a dark room (subject placed in a darkened room to dilate the pupils) or mydriatic provocative test (subject's pupils dilated with drops) may be performed. Significant rises in intraocular pressure indicate the likelihood of future spontaneous angle closure and may make preventive laser surgery advisable *(see page 98)*.

Fluorescein Angiography

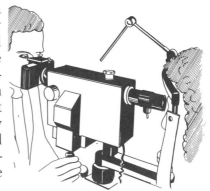

Fluorescein angiography is a specialized photographic study of the blood vessels, retina and other tissues in the back of the eye. Fluorescein "dye" is injected into one of the arm veins, circulates throughout the blood vessels of the body including those of the eye and provides for high contrast pictures of the inside of the eye with the "fundus camera".

Areas of blood vessel leakage and other vascular abnormalities in the back of the eye can be very clearly delineated by the use of this procedure. Diabetic retinopathy, exudative macular degeneration *(see page 175)* and blood vessel blockages are among the many ocular conditions that can be investigated by the use of fluorescein angiography. In most cases fluorescein angiography is a safe and simple test but allergic reactions sometimes occur and can very occasionally be serious.

Visual Field Testing

Vision testing normally involves measuring of the central visual acuity (see visual acuity testing, above). In certain instances it is also important to test the peripheral (or "side") vision.

This is usually accomplished with a computerized perimeter which is a hollow hemisphere into which the subject's head is positioned. A "fixation" target or spot is used to keep the individual looking straight ahead while a series of tiny faint lights are projected onto the inside of the bowl. In most current field testers the light intensity can be varied. Each time a light is perceived the subject presses a button and the computer "remembers" where in the hemisphere lights were seen or not and how intense the light had to be before it was detected. One eye is tested at a time.

Various print-outs of this information can be obtained including "gray scale" maps of the peripheral vision, numeric values of the "depth" of a blind spot, etc. This information can usually be stored in the computer and compared to the results of future testing to determine whether a condition is worsening or not. Precision manual perimeters (Goldmann perimeters) are also still in use in some offices and clinics.

Visual field testing can also be carried out with less sophisticated apparatus. In a routine exam setting, the ophthalmologist or other medical doctor may present small objects or even a waving hand to the subject while one eye is covered and the other is looking straight ahead. This means of testing called "confrontation" is useful for detecting gross visual field deficits. Another modality involves the use of a black screen (tangent screen) and white "test objects" or a battery operated "wand" with a tiny light at one end. The limits of the visual field for a certain size and brightness test object can be manually plotted.

The information obtained with visual field testing is invaluable to the proper management of glaucoma and in the detection of vision deficits in a number of neurologic disorders including strokes and optic neuritis.

Radiography (X-rays, CT Scans, etc.)

X-rays or "plain films" are very helpful in diagnosing various conditions affecting the eyes such as orbital tumors or fractures. etc. Skull and sinus films are also often indirectly helpful in the evaluation of some eye conditions and injuries.

A special form of computer summated X-ray called a CT or CAT scan (computerized tomography or computerized axial to-

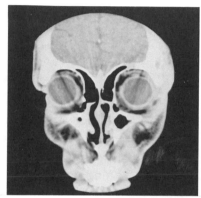

CT scan of head

mography) provides for enhanced, extremely well defined images for making subtle diagnoses.

A newer, highly sophisticated imaging procedure providing even better images than CT is now being widely used by ophthalmologists. The **MRI** (magnetic resonance imaging) scan uses magnetism as opposed to the x-radiation used in x-rays and CT scans.

Tear Testing

Tears can be both overproduced (e.g., inflammations, foreign bodies, crying, etc.) and underproduced (dry eye syndrome). In addition, the tear drainage system can be compromised in various ways causing excess tearing. In many cases the problem is quite obvious but other cases require sensitive diagnostic tests to sort things out.

In cases of dry eyes or deficient tearing, a Schirmer test is performed. This consists of inserting a small strip of special filter paper between the eye and the lower lid and measuring the amount of wetting of the strip in a five minute period. The test is often performed after instilling a topical anesthetic in the eye to eliminate the normal reflex tearing that might occur from the "foreign body" irritation of the strip. Results consistently below the accepted normal levels support the diagnosis of a true dry eye condition.

The "tear break up time" (BUT) is another simple test of tear function performed by the ophthalmologist observing at the slit lamp the time between a complete blink and the first dry spot developing in the tear film on the cornea. A rapid BUT is seen in "mucin deficient" dry eye states (relative deficiency of the mucus layer of tears).

There are, in addition, a number of other sophisticated laboratory analyses of the tears that can be performed in cases of suspected dry eye states *(see page 147)*.

In cases where tearing is excessive, the differentiation must be made between overproduction of tears and poor drainage. Various dye tests have been devised for this purpose and involve the recovery of stained tears from the nose as an indication that the drainage system is functioning normally.

Probing and irrigation of the tear ducts also provides information regarding the patency of the tear drainage system. In adults, this test is performed comfortably in the office.

A dacryocystogram is an X-ray of the orbit in the area of the tear ducts after the instillation of a radio-opaque dye into the tear drainage system. The exact site of a blockage in the system can be determined by this means.

Electrophysiologic Testing (ERG, EOG, VER)

The normal visual process involves electric potentials which can be measured in various ways. Some visual disorders manifest abnormalities in the normal electric potentials and can be diagnosed and monitored by this means.

The electroretinogram (ERG) is measured by placing a contact lens electrode on the eye and presenting the subject with a standardized flash of light. The change in the retina's electric potential is then recorded and measured. This test is usually performed in normal room light and again after the eye is "dark-adapted". The brightness, frequency and color of the flash can be varied to obtain more information.

The ERG is particularly useful in diagnosing and monitoring the hereditary chorioretinal diseases such as retinitis pigmentosa and its variants. Various retinal circulatory and toxic disorders can also be monitored by the ERG. In cases where there is unexplained visual loss, certain cases of ocular trauma and prior to some eye operations, the ERG can provide valuable information regarding the status of the retina. The electrooculogram

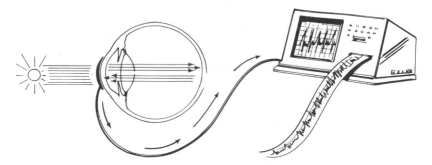

(EOG) tests a different aspect of the eye's electric activity and has more limited use than the ERG.

The visual evoked response (VER or VEP—visual evoked potential) assesses the integrity of the entire visual system from the eye to the visual cortex of the brain *(see pages 6 and 11)*. Various ocular and neurologic abnormalities can be detected and monitored by this means.

The test is usually performed with the subject looking at a shifting checkerboard pattern on a video screen while the electric activity so generated is recorded from electrodes attached to the back of the skull near the visual cortex of the brain. The main contributors to the VER are the macula (center of retina) and the optic nerve. Significant disorders of either of these elements will produce an abnormal VER. The VER can even be used in infants to test for amblyopia *(see page 126)*.

TESTS OF EYE MUSCLE COORDINATION

There are a total of twelve tiny muscles (six to each eye) controlling the movements of the eyes. Normally a delicate balance is maintained assuring that the eyes remain parallel in all directions of gaze. In some cases, when the balance is upset for any reason, the resulting deviation of one or both eyes is readily apparent (see strabismus, page 199). In many other cases, however, the imbalance may be very subtle requiring special tests to detect and measure the deviation. In either case, knowing that there is a deviation is only the first step in diagnosis and management. It is also critical to know the exact type and degree of misalignment and the nature of the brain's adaptations to this misalignment. Some of the major tests of eye muscle coordination are discussed below:

Cover tests

By placing a cover (usu-
ally a black plastic spoon-
shaped object) in front of
one or the other eye, a
great deal about the alignment and coordination of
the eyes can be deter-
mined. The cross cover test
involves alternating the
cover in front of one eye
and then the other while
the subject looks at a "fixation target". This maneuver
interrupts the normal "fu-
sion mechanism" of the eyes whereby the two eyes are kept
aligned on an object. Any tendency that the eyes may have to
drift to a "position of rest" *(see phorias, pages 154 and 158)* will
be elicited by this test.

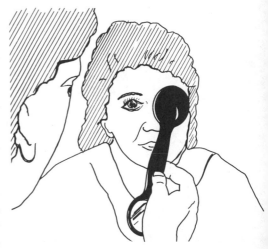

The cover/uncover test is used to detect actual misalignments of the eyes *(see tropias, pages 154 and 160)*. In this test,
the cover is placed in front of one eye and then removed. This is
repeated a number of times to the examiner's satisfaction. The
other eye is then usually tested in a similar fashion. If, for example, the right eye is turning slightly inward toward the nose,
placing the cover in front of the left eye will cause the right eye
to make a slight movement outward to realign this eye on the
object of regard. This is an extremely sensitive means of determining whether there is an actual misalignment of the eyes even
when the misalignment is very slight. The prism and cover tests
allow for measuring of the amount of turn or misalignment.

Range of motion test

Normally the eyes are capable
of moving in all directions while
remaining aligned and parallel
with each other. By simply di-
recting the subject to follow a
small light or other target, the
ophthalmologist can determine
whether the eyes are either restricted or overacting in various
directions of gaze.

Red glass test

In this test, a red lens or glass is placed in front of one eye as the subject views a small white light ("muscle light"). If the eyes are misaligned and the vision in both eyes is intact (no suppression or amblyopia) the subject will see two separate lights, a red one and a white one. The degree of separation of the two lights may vary in different directions of gaze depending on the nature of the misalignment.

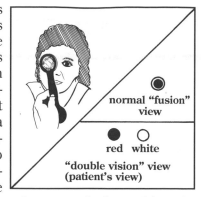

Sometimes a red glass with striations (red Maddox rod) is used to make the two images more discernable. Prisms can also be used to measure the degree of separation of the two images and thus the degree of misalignment of the eyes.

Worth 4-dot test (red/green glasses)

This test involves the use of a special pair of glasses with one red glass and one green glass. An array of red, green and white lights is placed in front of the subject who then tells the examiner the number and color of lights he sees. In cases of suppression of vision in one eye, the lights of one color will not be seen. In cases of double vision "extra" lights will be seen and in cases of normal "fusion", the correct diamond-shaped, multicolored array will be identified.

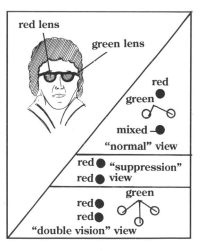

Stereopsis (depth perception) testing

Special polarized glasses and a "3-D" target are used in this test to assess the degree to which the two eyes can cooperate to create a three dimensional image. Individuals with poor eye muscle coordination, suppres-

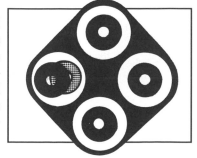

sion and amblyopia, etc. do not perceive depth normally and may have difficulty judging distances and coordinating fine hand-eye movements. The stereo tests help to identify these individuals and can also quantify the degree of depth perception (stereoacuity).

There are many other special tests of eye muscle alignment and coordination that the ophthalmologist may use but the tests described above are the ones most commonly used in an office setting.

Color Vision Testing

Color blindness, where one sees only shades of gray, is an extremely rare disorder. Much more common are the inherited red/green color deficiencies. Eight to ten percent of males and one half to one percent of females are red or green color deficient. Individuals with these defects in color perception tend to confuse reds and greens. Blue/yellow color deficiencies are quite rare. Color vision deficiencies can also be acquired due to certain disorders of the optic nerve and retina.

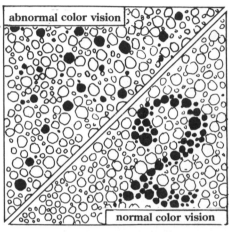

The most commonly used in-office color vision tests are the Ishihara and the Hardy-Rand-Rittler pseudoisochromatic plates. These test color vision with colored test symbols within different colored backgrounds. The symbols are not seen normally by color deficient individuals who confuse the various colors.

There are several other more subtle color tests (Farnsworth Munsell, etc.) which are used in research and for qualification for certain jobs and services.

Amsler Grid

Amsler, a Swiss ophthalmologist developed a series of lined and patterned grids for testing the central twenty degrees of the visual field. These plates are also very useful for detecting, outlining and documenting distortions in the central vision due to

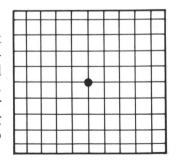

various macular disorders especially exudative macular degeneration *(see page 175)*. The most commonly used grid appears on the inside of the back cover.

After covering one eye, the subject is asked to look at the central fixation dot and to describe any areas of the grid that appear to be distorted, or interrupted. The fellow eye is then tested in a similar fashion. Distorted areas can be outlined for documentation and future comparison.

Certain predisposed individuals (especially those with exudative macular degeneration in the fellow eye) are advised to post an Amsler grid where they will conveniently see it daily and to test the eyes themselves and report any abnormalities to their ophthalmologist promptly.

Interferometry

The ophthalmologist must often determine how much of a patient's reduced vision is due to a cataract versus a coexisting ocular disorder such as macular degeneration. If, for example, ninety percent of the lost vision resulted from the cataract and only ten percent from the macular degeneration, then cataract surgery would be an appropriate course of action. Interferometry provides a means for making this determination.

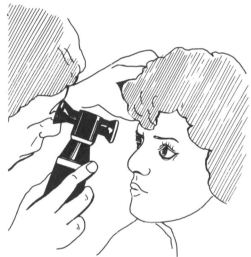

Very finely focused beams of light (in some cases laser light) are used to penetrate the cataract and project a pattern onto the retina. The spacing between the lines of the pattern can be varied by the examiner and an estimate of the potential visual acuity can be obtained by recording the smallest separation between the lines that the subject can discriminate.

Other devices such as the PAM (potential acuity meter) are available for the same purpose. It should be stressed that the results of these tests are estimates only and the resultant visual acuity after cataract surgery may be greater or lesser than these predictions.

Miscellaneous Diagnostic Modalities

Laboratory tests (blood tests, skin tests, cultures, etc.) are commonly used by the ophthalmologist to help diagnose various conditions affecting the eyes and/or the general health.

Biopsies are surgical procedures whereby part or all of a lesion (growth, tumor, etc.) is removed and sent to the pathology laboratory for examination under a microscope to determine its exact nature and malignant potential.

Carotid artery blood flow studies are often performed (usually by other specialists) to evaluate the circulation of blood to the brain and eyes. This information can prove valuable in the prevention of strokes.

What to Expect From a Medical Eye Examination

A complete, uncomplicated medical eye examination includes but is not limited to the following:

- establishment of the chief complaint(s) and detailing of the pertinent past medical and ocular history
- determination of the prescription of any current eye glasses
- measurement of visual acuity (with/without glasses at far and close range depending on the circumstances)
- external examination
- refraction (in young children, in patients with strabismus and in the mentally deficient, cyclopegic/mydriatic drops are usually required—*see page 84*)
- tonometry (not usually necessary in children—may be performed with "air puff", applanation, or both—applanation requires use of drops)
- pupil evaluation
- motility evaluation (eye muscle function)
- slit lamp examination
- ophthalmoscopy (may be performed with or without the use of dilating drops, depending on the circumstances and physician preference). When only anesthetic drops are used during the exam (for applanation tonometry), there is no resultant blurring of the vision—the eyes will simply feel

---

slightly "numb" for about five minutes. When dilating drops are used, vision may be blurred, especially at close range for several hours depending on the nature and strength of the drops used.

The pupils may remain dilated from hours to, occasionally, a day or so.

Other tests are preformed as indicated by the results of the "core" examination. As mentioned above, technical and nursing staff may assist the ophthalmologist in the evaluation of the eyes.

Subsequent short exams for specific purposes often only require one or a few of the above mentioned "core" tests.

THE EYES AS WINDOWS ON YOUR HEALTH

Examination of the eyes can reveal a great deal about one's general health. It is not uncommon for the ophthalmologist to discover a generalized ailment in the course of a routine eye examination. It should be understood, however, that the absence of eye involvement does not exclude the possibility of generalized medical disease.

Following is a summary of some of the more commonly encountered medical disorders which may have ophthalmic manifestations. The medical disorder is indicated in bold letters followed by some of the possible associated ocular findings. Many of the findings can occur in other disease states and are not specific for the condition being described. *For further details on these conditions, consult the Encyclopedia of Ocular Disorders section, page 125).*

Anemia *(low blood count)*
- pallor of the palpebral conjunctiva (lining of the inside of the lid)
- retinal hemorrhages
- retinal infarcts ("cotton wool patches"—areas of cloudy swelling of the retina due to nerve cell damage
- other findings specific to certain types of anemia

Arteriosclerosis *(hardening or stiffening of arteries)*
- arteriosclerotic retinopathy
- retinal vein occlusions

Arthritis *(see Rheumatoid arthritis, page 53)*

Atherorosclerosis *(fatty & connective tissue deposits inside vessels)*
- retinal artery occlusions

Brain tumors
- papilledema (swelling of the optic nerves from increased intra-cranial pressure)
- cranial nerve palsies (e.g., double vision, limited motion of eyes, etc.)
- visual field defects (partial loss of side vision)
- pupillary abnormalities

Cancer
- metastases (spread) from many different primary tumors originating in other parts of the body may be seen in the eyes or orbits, etc.

Carotid artery insufficiency *(inadequate blood flow through major neck arteries)*
- amaurosis fugax (fleeting loss of vision)
- retinal artery occlusions
- retinal artery emboli (tiny cholesterol and calcium chips in retinal arterioles)

Diabetes mellitus *("sugar diabetes")*
- refractive changes (usually increased nearsightedness or decreased farsightedness)
- diabetic retinopathy
- rubeosis iridis (abnormal blood vessels on the iris)
- eye muscle paralyses
- cataracts

Drug toxicities
- many drugs, both prescribed and illicit may have effects on the eyes which can be discovered during a routine eye exam

Hypercholesterolemia *(high blood cholesterol)*
- xanthelasma of lids
- arcus senilis (white ring on cornea)

Hyperparathyroidism *(overacting parathyroid gland)*
- band keratopathy (calcium deposits on cornea)

Hypertension (high blood pressure)
- hypertensive retinopathy
- papilledema
- subconjunctival hemorrhages

Hyperthyroidism (overacting thyroid gland)
- proptosis (exophthalmos, bulging of the eyes)
- lid retraction (upper lid elevated higher than normal)
- "thyroid stare" (infrequent blinking)
- optic nerve compression
- eye muscle abnormalities
- exposure keratitis

Hypoparathyroidism (underacting parathyroid gland)
- cataracts
- keratitis and conjunctivitis

Hypothyroidism (underacting thyroid gland)
- eyelid swelling (doughy skin)
- loss of eye brows (outer one third)
- may see proptosis, etc., as above when pre-existing hyperthyroidism has been treated and thyroid hormone levels are low or normal

Infectious diseases (the following is a list of general categories of systemic infectious diseases [i.e., transmitted by microorganisms] that can be manifested in the eyes. There are, in addition many other primary infections that originate in the eyes.)
- bacterial infections (such as gonorrhea, botulism, subacute bacterial endocarditis, etc.)
- viral infections (such as mumps, measles, chicken pox, cytomegalovirus, influenza, AIDS, herpes simplex and herpes zoster, etc.)
- mycobacterial infections (such as tuberculosis, etc.)
- fungal infections (such as histoplasmosis, etc.)
- protozoan infections (such as toxoplasmosis)
- spirochetal infections (such as syphilis, etc.)
- rickettsial infections (such as Rocky mountain spotted fever, typhus, etc.)
- various worm infestations (not uncommon in some third world countries)

Juvenile rheumatoid arthritis (JRA, Still's disease)
- iritis
- band keratopathy (calcium deposits on cornea)
- cataracts

Kidney disorders
- renal failure can be manifested in the retina and retinal blood vessels
- various hereditary kidney disorders may have ocular manifestations

Leukemia ("cancer" of white blood cells)
- subconjunctival hemorrhages
- leukemic retinopathy

Liver disease (cirrhosis, hepatitis, etc.)
- scleral icterus (whites of eyes become yellow or jaundiced)
- night blindness (secondary to vitamin A deficiency)

Lupus (systemic lupus erythematosis, SLE)
- dry eyes (keratoconjunctivitis sicca, Sjogren's syndrome)
- episcleritis and scleritis
- lupus retinopathy

Multiple sclerosis (demyelinating disease)
- optic (retrobulbar) neuritis
- nystagmus
- internuclear ophthalmoplegia (uncoordinated eye movements)
- cranial nerve palsies

Myasthenia gravis
- ptosis (droopy eye lid(s), usually worse later in the day)
- extraocular muscle weaknesses (double vision)

Phakomatoses (group of conditions with cutaneous (skin), neurologic and ocular findings—can often be diagnosed by an eye exam)
- Sturge Weber
- neurofibromatosis (Von Recklinghausen's disease)
- tuberous sclerosis
- von Hippel-Lindau
- Wyburn Mason
- ataxia telangiectasia

Polycythemia *(excessive quantity of blood cells)*
- retinal vein occlusions
- swollen conjunctival blood vessels
- retinal hemorrhages

Rheumatoid arthritis
- dry eyes (keratoconjunctivitis sicca, Sjogren's syndrome)
- episcleritis and scleritis
- corneal/limbal ulcerations and perforations

Sarcoidosis *(Boeck's sarcoid)*
- uveitis
- conjunctival lesions
- iris nodules
- sarcoid retinopathy
- lacrimal gland inflammation
- optic neuritis
- cranial nerve palsies

Skeletal disorders
- Marfan's syndrome (can cause retinal detachments, dislocated lens, etc.)
- osteogenesis imperfecta (can cause blue sclera, cataracts., etc.)

Skin disorders
- acne rosacea (can cause keratitis, conjunctivitis, blepharitis, etc.)
- icthyosis (can cause ectropion, corneal lesions, etc.)
- psoriasis (can cause blepharitis, conjunctivitis, uveitis, etc.)
- pseudoxanthoma elasticum (can cause angioid streaks of the retina)

Stroke *(cerebrovascular accident, CVA)*
- loss of vision (may be partial or complete, temporary or permanent usually one sided or on one side of the visual field of both eyes)
- cranial nerve palsies (e.g., double vision, limited motion of eyes, etc.)
- pupillary abnormalities

Temporal arteritis (cranial arteritis, giant cell arteritis)
- ischemic optic neuropathy
- cranial nerve palsies
- central retinal artery occlusion

Ulcerative colitis and regional ileitis
- iritis and episcleritis

Vitamin disorders
- both vitamin deficiencies and excesses can be manifested in the eyes
- vitamin C deficiency (scurvy)—ocular hemorrhages
- vitamin B12 deficiency (pernicious anemia)—optic neuritis, retinopathy of anemia
- thiamine deficiency (beri-beri)—cranial nerve palsies, etc.
- vitamin A deficiency—night blindness, dry eyes and corneal damage
- vitamin A toxicity—papilledema, double vision
- vitamin D toxicity—band keratopathy (calcium deposits on cornea)

The eyes can also manifest side effects and toxicities from various medications being used for treatment of other disorders. For example, steroids ("cortisone") can cause cataracts and elevated intraocular pressure. Some tranquilizers can cause focusing problems and retinal damage. Some medications used to treat arthritis and lupus can cause retinal damage and a new cholesterol-lowering drug has been reported to cause cataracts.

Your ophthalmologist will be able to detect these abnormalities and confer with the treating doctor regarding possible changes in medication.

TREATMENT

Total eye care consists of *optical, medical* and *surgical* care. Optical care includes the prescription of glasses, contact lenses and low vision aids. The dispensing of these optical aids is ordinarily carried out by an optician or optometrist. Medical care consists of the use of eye drops and eye ointments as well as oral and other forms of medication. Surgical care involves operations on or around the eyes using lasers or standard surgical techniques.

The ophthalmologist is uniquely qualified to deliver all forms of eye care and, through special training and experience, chooses the proper combination of treatments to best address the problem at hand.

In the following sections an overview and explanation of the most common forms of eye care will be presented. The reader is urged to use this material for the purpose of information and explanation and should not engage in any form of self diagnosis or treatment. Serious damage to the eyes can result from the improper management of ocular disorders. The only exception is in cases of emergency—guidelines for the proper handling of accidents and injuries are given at the end of this section.

OPTICAL TREATMENT

Spectacle Lenses

Disturbances in vision caused by refractive disorders are most commonly corrected through the use of spectacle lenses. Various types of plastics and glasses are utilized in the manufacture of today's spectacle lenses.

Glass lenses tend to be heavier than plastic lenses and they resist scratches more effectively than conventional plastic lenses. Because the index of refraction of glass is greater than plastic, glass lenses tend to be slightly thinner. This is only apparent in very strong prescriptions. Various types of glass are currently used in spectacle lenses. Crown glass is used most commonly. High-Lite® (Schott Glass Technologies, Inc.) is a glass material with an even higher index of refraction thus making the lens even thinner. Photochromic glass is impregnated with silver halide crystals which, when exposed to ultraviolet light, darken to decrease light transmission. These lenses are available in grey or brown. With lower levels of ultraviolet light, the lenses lighten to almost clear glass.

Plastic lenses have gained increasing popularity due to their light weight (50% of glass). Conventional plastics have a tendency to scratch but recent advances have resulted in different materials which are highly resistant to scratching (RLX Plus® [Armorlite], Super Shield® [Silor Optical, Inc.], etc.). Plastic lenses are more impact resistant than are glass lenses and tend to fog less when there is a sudden change in temperature. Antireflection coating may be applied to plastic lenses to reduce reflection which is noticeable in strong prescriptions. Polycarbonate plastics are available in safety lenses which provide maximum protection from high velocity particle impact. Plastics with a higher index of refraction are now available so that thickness is dramatically reduced in strong prescriptions. Plastic lenses, like glass, can also be tinted any number of shades.

Optical Correction Of Refractive Disorders

Myopia (nearsightedness) is a condition in which light from a distant object focuses *in front of* the retina and thus appears blurry to the individual. To correct this condition, a *concave* lens is placed before the eye such that the focus of light falls on the retina. A concave lens is thin in the center and thick at the edges *(see below)*.

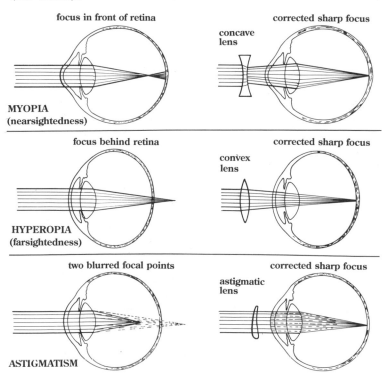

focus in front of retina   corrected sharp focus

concave lens

MYOPIA (nearsightedness)

focus behind retina   corrected sharp focus

convex lens

HYPEROPIA (farsightedness)

two blurred focal points   corrected sharp focus

astigmatic lens

ASTIGMATISM

Hyperopia (farsightedness) is a condition in which light focuses *behind* the retina. Objects, especially at close range, are not clearly seen without a focusing effort. To correct this condition, a *convex* lens is placed before the eyes such that the focus of light falls on the retina. A convex lens is thin at the edges and thicker in the center *(see page 56)*.

Astigmatism is a condition in which light from an object actually focuses at two separate points in the eye. These points may both be in front of the retina, both behind the retina or straddle the retina. Vision is usually blurred to some degree at all ranges. The correction for astigmatism requires a lens which has different powers along different axes *(see page 56)*. This is known as a *cylindrical lens*. This type of lens brings both points of focus into one point directly at the retina. This lens will usually have one edge thicker than the other edge.

Presbyopia is the natural condition in which, due to aging, the crystalline lens loses its elasticity and thus cannot focus on nearby objects. This condition is corrected with a convex lens in addition to any appropriate distance correction so as to focus light from nearby objects onto the retina. This form of correction may require the use of two separate pairs of glasses, one for distance and another for near, or the use of bifocals (one pair of glasses with both distance and near lenses). Other types of multifocal lenses (trifocals and progressive adds) will be discussed below.

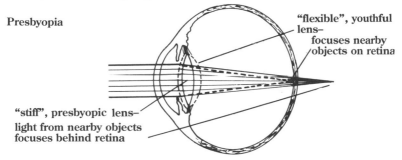

Presbyopia

"flexible", youthful lens– focuses nearby objects on retina

"stiff", presbyopic lens– light from nearby objects focuses behind retina

Forms of Visual Correction

Single vision spectacles are lenses which are used to correct one visual problem; e.g., myopia, hyperopia, astigmatism. These eyeglasses are generally used for only one task; e.g., distance vision or near vision. This is by far the most common form of visual correction.

Multifocal spectacles are lenses which are used to correct a combination of visual problems, e.g., presbyopia coexisting with the need for a distance correction. There are many forms of multifocals available: bifocals, trifocals, blended bifocals, progressive add lens, and occupational lenses.

Types of bifocals include: Flat Top, Kryptok, Executive, A-Ultex, and Roundtop.

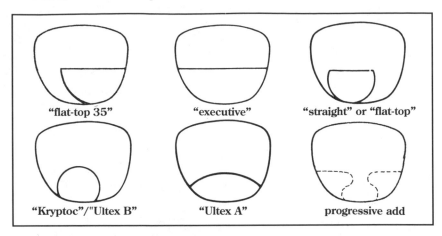

| "flat-top 35" | "executive" | "straight" or "flat-top" |
| "Kryptoc"/"Ultex B" | "Ultex A" | progressive add |

Flat Top lenses are the most common. The width of the segment (lower reading portion) may be made 22 mm, 25 mm, 28 mm or 35 mm depending on the individual's lifestyle and visual needs.

Executive lenses have a segment which extends across the entire length of the lens. This is a popular lens with individuals who require a wide field of view at close range.

Kryptok lenses are an older style and rarely used except for individuals who are currently wearing them and do not desire to change. The reading segment is 22 mm wide in this type of bifocal.

A-Ultex lenses are also an older style which are rarely used today. The reading segment is a maximum of 40 mm at the widest point of the segment, but decreases toward the top.

Trifocals are lenses with three different zones for focusing light. These lenses are commonly available in the Flat Top version or the Executive version. The top portion of the lens is used for viewing distance objects, the middle zone is used for viewing objects at an intermediate distance (i.e., 18 inches to 36 inches on average) and the lower zone is used for viewing objects at the usual reading range.

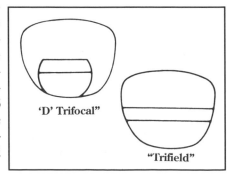

'D' Trifocal"

"Trifield"

Blended bifocals are generally Kryptok bifocals in which the junction between distance and near segments is polished. This zone of polishing masks the fact that the individual is wearing bifocals, but it often causes a zone of distorted vision which may distract some individuals.

Progressive Addition Lenses are lenses which provide for multiple different points of focus. The top portion of the lens is used for viewing distant objects. The lower portion of the lens is used for reading and other near tasks. Between the two is a "corridor" in which the prescription is gradually changed from distance vision to near vision. The lens thus has a vast number of focal points allowing for clear, comfortable vision at all ranges.

Occupational lenses are lenses designed specifically for tasks of a particular occupation. Such lenses may have an additional segment placed at the top of the lens such that near point tasks are easily seen when looking up (auto mechanics, electricians, plumbers, librarians etc.). Lenses may also be prescribed such that the intermediate zone in a trifocal is very large for use with computer terminals, for example.

Absorptive Lenses and Coatings

Both plastic and glass lenses may be made in a variety of colors for various purposes.

Glass lenses may be tinted by two methods. One is by the addition of a coating onto a clear lens. The coating may be any color desired. As it is only a coating, it may be scratched or worn off. The lens color will have a uniform density regardless of lens prescription. Glass lenses may also be impregnated to achieve a desired color. Certain chemicals are added to the lens material during its manufacture, such that the desired color is achieved. Impregnated tints will not wear off, but may appear darker or lighter in certain areas of the lens depending upon the lens prescription and thickness.

Plastic lenses are tinted by placing the lens in a hot dye which is absorbed at the lens surface to achieve a desired effect. The density of the color is determined by the length of time the lens remains in contact with the solution. The tint may fade slightly with time.

Photochromic lenses darken in bright light and become clear in the dark. These are ordinarily made of glass but a newer plastic version is now available.

CARE & MAINTENANCE

Color selection is a personal matter, although tints which filter ultraviolet radiation are strongly recommended. Neutral density lenses are non-selective and thus decrease the transmission of all wavelengths of light. These lenses are usually somewhat gray in color. Selective absorbers are lenses which selectively decrease the transmission of certain wavelengths (colors) of light. Ultraviolet absorbers tend to be yellow-orange in color. Polarized lenses are lenses which transmit light in one direction only and can significantly reduce glare. Special tints are used for industrial purposes to absorb certain wavelengths which may cause damage to the eye (welding arcs, lasers, torches, etc.). Lenses can also be tinted in a "gradient" fashion with a darker tint at the top of the lens as compared with the bottom.

Antireflective coatings can be used to decrease the number of bothersome internal reflections in plastic lenses which coincidentally makes stronger, thicker prescriptions appear less obvious. Scratch resistant coatings, as mentioned above, can also be applied but generally not together with antireflective coatings.

Ophthalmic Dispensing *(the art of eye glass fitting)*

When eyeglasses are dispensed, it is important that they be placed correctly in front of the eyes. After initial frame selection, the individual's pupillary distance (space between the eyes) is measured for both distance and near. It is imperative that the optical center of the lens be placed directly in line with the individual's pupils. Failure to do so will cause uncomfortable vision or, if considerably misaligned, double vision.

Bifocal heights must also be carefully measured. The reading segment should not be set so high as to interfere with distance vision, nor too low where it may prevent comfortable near vision.

Frame adjustment is also critical to comfortable vision. Frames should be adjusted such that the lenses have a slight tilt with the top portion of the lens slightly further from the eye than the bottom portion. The frame should also have a small degree of "face-form" tilt.

Special prism corrections are sometimes incorporated to compensate for eye muscle imbalances *(see Double Vision, page 146)*. In bifocals of very unequal strength lenses, a special compensation is sometimes made in one lens to avoid double vision ("slab-off" correction).

Basic Eyewear Care

For many years, simple crown glass and plastic (cr-39) were the only materials used for spectacle lenses. Both were cleaned with soap (dishwashing liquid) and water and dried with a soft cloth or tissue. Rinsing plastic lenses with water prior to cleaning is recommended to remove any clinging debris which would otherwise scratch the lens surface.

These basic cleaning methods are still recommended today but several new lens materials and coatings are available requiring some alteration of cleaning procedures.

Polycarbonate (plastic), though very durable, can not be cleaned with acetone (nail polish remover and other strong solvents) as it dissolves lens surfaces.

Scratch coated lenses should be cleaned several times per day to keep oils from the skin and acids from wearing the coating away.

Anti-reflective coatings allow more light to pass through the lens. The reflections from television and computer screens, streetlights, and headlights, etc. are virtually eliminated. Although this is a very useful coating, it can be quite fragile requiring the use of special anti-reflective cleaners (liquid products) and special cloths to polish the surfaces between cleanings.

For most other lenses, soap and water provide the safest and most economical means of lens cleaning. If any lens deposits remain after cleaning, the glasses should be brought to the optician for evaluation.

Anti-fog and anti-static lens cleaning solutions are also available for situations requiring their use.

Frames

All metal and plastic frames should be washed with soap and water then rinsed and dried to keep them looking new. Soap and water may not remove debris trapped between the lens and frame. The optician or other dispensing professional can disassemble the frame to allow for complete manual or ultrasonic cleaning.

Other Simple Tips on on Proper Eyewear Care

- the use of a proper case can greatly extend the life of your eyewear
- use two hands when putting on or removing your glasses to help keep the frame in proper alignment and to minimize breakage
- never place your glasses on a table lens-surface-down—this invites scratches
- do not attempt to make your own frame adjustments—consult your optician or dispensing professional
- a note on "scratch resistant lenses"—there is no *scratch-proof* lens—*all* lenses can be scratched—common sense and care are necessary when handling eyewear
- your old eyewear can be donated to charities—consult your optician or dispensing professional for details

Contact Lenses

Contact lenses are another form of visual correction. They are made from various synthetic materials designed to float comfortably on the layer of tears covering the cornea. The inner surface of the contact lens is composed of various curves which permit the contact lens to center on the cornea so as to allow for clear comfortable vision.

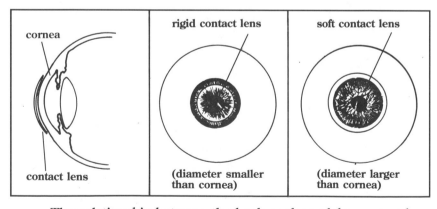

cornea

contact lens

rigid contact lens

(diameter smaller than cornea)

soft contact lens

(diameter larger than cornea)

The relationship between the back surface of the contact lens and the cornea is critical. Tears must flow freely between the contact lens and the cornea to provide for metabolic waste removal and good corneal nutrition. The outer surface of the contact lens must be designed to make the contact lens comfortable as well as to provide optical correction to improve visual acuity.

Many individuals wear contact lenses for cosmetic reasons, however, contacts can also provide better vision for certain visual tasks (e.g., sports, special occupational needs, etc.) or to treat certain ocular conditions, e.g., keratoconus.

Contact lenses are now available to correct all types of refractive errors such as myopia, hyperopia, astigmatism, aphakia, and presbyopia. A thorough eye examination is always required prior to determining if one is a candidate for contact lens wear. The single most important criterion for successfully wearing contact lenses is *motivation*. The ideal candidate is one who has a healthy cornea with an adequate tear film who is highly motivated. Poor candidates include those individuals with chronic infections of the lids or cornea, individuals with dry eyes, those who cannot physically manipulate the contact lens, and those who have a fear of wearing contact lenses.

Age is not a major consideration in deciding whether to prescribe contact lenses. As long as the individual is mature enough to understand and comply with the recommendations for insertion, removal and care of the lenses, contacts can usually be worn safely and effectively. The only other consideration with regard to age is the stability of the refractive error. Prescription changes are often quite frequent in youngsters and teenagers requiring continued follow-up and updating of the contact lenses.

One must always weigh the advantages and the disadvantages of contact lens wear. Advantages include greater field of vision, increased self-confidence, elimination of pressure points on nose and ears from glasses, more realistic size of viewed objects, and elimination of fogged eyeglass lenses from rain and perspiration. The disadvantages include adaptation and handling difficulties for some individuals as well as the necessity for regular care and good ocular hygiene.

There are essentially three different materials from which contact lenses are made. They include polymethyl methacrylate (PMMA) in hard contact lenses, various hydrogel plastic polymers in the case of soft lenses and other types of plastic and silicone or fluoride materials in the case of gas permeable ("semi-soft") lenses. Every manufacturer of contact lenses uses slight variations in the above named materials to produce their particular lenses. Lenses of the three basic types may be designed to correct all the different refractive errors.

Hard Contact Lenses

Hard contact lenses do not flex on the cornea. They transmit no oxygen and therefore, must move with each blink so as to provide nourishment to the cornea and to dispose of metabolic wastes. These lenses tend to be small in diameter (8-10 mm) and are often tinted to aid in handling the lens as well as to enhance a patient's natural eye color.

The back surfaces of these lenses are custom designed by the doctor so as to have an optimal fitting relationship with the individual's cornea. Hard contact lenses are preferred for individuals with large degrees of astigmatism.

A major disadvantage of hard contact lenses is that they can deprive the cornea of adequate amounts of oxygen and thus cause corneal edema (swelling) leading to decreased visual acuity. This blurred vision often lasts for hours following the removal of the contact lens, but is reversible once adequate amounts of oxygen are provided to the cornea. Gas permeable lenses were developed to eliminate this problem with hard contact lenses. Hard lenses are also more commonly associated with corneal irritations and abrasions and "contact lens overwear syndrome". Hard lenses are also more likely than soft lenses to be lost from the eye during sports, or other rough activity.

Hard lenses are, however, quite durable, easy to care for, and provide excellent visual acuity for most or all of the wearing period.

Gas Permeable ("semi-soft") Contact Lenses

Gas permeable lenses are similar in design to hard contact lenses. They tend to flex more due to their chemical composition. The range of color availability of gas permeable contact lenses is somewhat limited. The major advantage of gas permeable lenses is that they transmit oxygen directly through the lens to the cornea. As a result, the cornea rarely becomes swollen and clear vision is maintained. Initial adaptation is also easier due to the greater oxygen transmission. Recent advances in polymer technology have produced gas permeable lenses which transmit enough oxygen to allow for use on an extended wear basis. Gas permeable lenses are easy to care for and tend to last for 2-5 years before replacement is necessary.

Soft Contact Lenses

Soft contact lenses are large, flexible lenses which, when hydrated, are composed of 38-80% water. They are very comfortable and are fit so that the edge of the contact lens actually extends beyond the boundary of the cornea onto the conjunctiva *(see page 62)*.

Comfort and ease of adaptation are the obvious advantages of soft contact lenses. The disadvantages of this type of lens include increased fragility, increased incidence of protein and mucus build-up on the lens and the need for greater care and maintenance. Very thin versions of this lens as well as lenses with very high water content can be used on an extended wear basis, being left on the eye for a number of days. Disposable soft contact lenses are also available. These lenses can be worn on a daily wear basis in which case they are cleaned and disinfected daily and then discarded after two weeks of wear. They can also be worn on an extended wear basis in which case they are worn for one week without removal and then discarded. Soft contact lenses are also available on a "planned replacement" schedule. These lenses are designed to be worn on a daily wear basis for one, three, or six months before they are discarded. The advantage of disposable wear or planned relacement lenses is the reduced protein, calcium and mucus build-up on the lens.

Soft contact lenses can also be designed to correct astigmatism. Recent advances in design have also made it possible for patients in need of bifocals to be fit with soft contact lenses. Tints are also available which enhance eye color as well as change eye color.

Contact Lens Fitting

After a thorough medical history and eye exam, the actual fitting of any type of contact lens involves a careful measurement of the individual's cornea. This is done by using an instrument known as a keratometer or ophthalmometer *(see page 33)*. This instrument measures corneal curvature and thus influences the selection of the type of contact lens best suited for the individual. Those with large degrees of corneal astigmatism are best fit with gas permeable or hard contact lenses. Individuals with less corneal astigmatism do well with soft contact lenses. A careful refraction to measure the exact prescription of the eye is, of course, also performed.

At this point, a contact lens is placed on the individual's eye based upon the initial measurements. The lens is allowed to settle on the eye for a period of 10-20 minutes. This lens is merely a trial lens and may not be of the correct prescription. An "over-refraction" is performed to determine the exact prescription and "best corrected visual acuity." The lens fit is then evaluated using the slit lamp *(see page 31)*. In the case of hard contact lenses and gas permeable lenses, special fluorescein eye drops are used to assess the adequacy of the fit . The lens should center well and move on the cornea slightly with each blink.

Any modifications in the lens fit are made based upon the doctor's observations. Once the proper fit is achieved and the individual is comfortable with the lenses, the exact parameters of

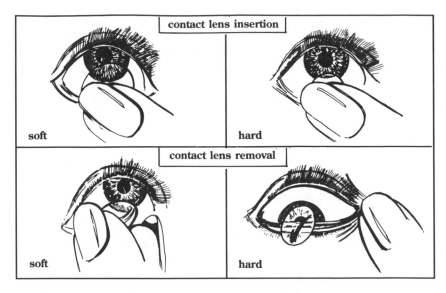

contact lens insertion	
soft	hard

contact lens removal	
soft	hard

the lenses are ordered from the appropriate manufacturer or dispensed from an inventory of stock lenses.

When the final lenses are received, the individual is carefully instructed on insertion, removal and care of the lenses. A wearing schedule appropriate to the individual is formulated by the doctor. During the initial adaptation period (approximately two weeks) the doctor should be notified about any adverse consequences from lens wear, e.g., pain, redness, decreased vision, etc. Assuming no discomfort, a two week check-up is scheduled with the doctor. At this visit, visual acuity is checked and proper fit is verified. Subjective complaints are also dealt with at this time. The individual is then advised to increase wearing time to the maximum period desired or the maximum advised by the doctor. A one-month follow up is then scheduled to evaluate the lens fit and visual acuity again. If no difficulties arise, semi-annual or annual follow-ups are advised. In the case of extended wear lenses, follow-up visits are usually more frequent.

Care and Maintenance of Contact Lenses

Caring for contact lenses involves two basic steps, regardless of the type of lens being used, namely, cleaning and lens disinfection. Cleaning involves the use of a detergent or cleaner to remove dirt, pollen, oils, make-up, etc. from the surface of the lens. Disinfection renders the lens free from bacteria, fungi, and viruses which may cause infection.

The lens is first removed from the eye and placed in the palm of the hand. Two drops of the daily cleaner solution are placed on the lens. The lens is mechanically cleaned by gently rubbing

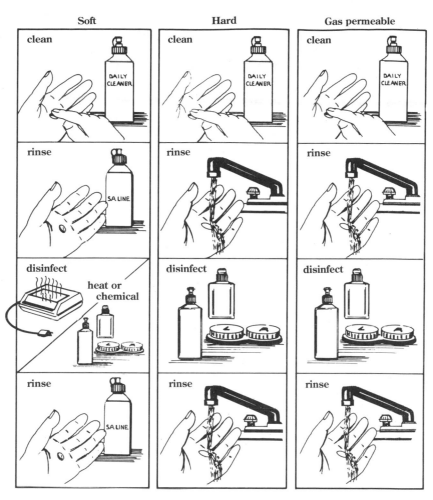

it with the index finger being careful not to damage the lens. In the case of hard contact lenses and gas permeable lenses, the cleaner is removed from the surface of the lens by the use of ordinary tap water. With soft contact lenses, the cleaner is removed by using a steady stream of saline solution.

At this point, the lenses are clean, but not sterile. Sterilization is achieved by either heat or chemicals. With hard contact lenses or gas permeable lenses, the process is always chemical. The lenses are placed in a case and filled with a chemical disinfection or storage solution. Complete disinfection usually takes a minimum time of four hours. The lenses may remain in the disinfecting solution, undisturbed, for an unlimited amount of time. Soft contact lenses can be heat or chemically disinfected. In the heat system, the lenses are placed in a case after cleaning and the case is filled with saline solution. The case is then placed in a heating unit which heats the lenses to a certain temperature, for a fixed amount of time. The unit then shuts off automatically. The lenses may remain in the case undisturbed until they are to be worn again. There are many different types of heat sterilization units available today.

Chemical disinfection of soft contact lenses may be achieved either by the conventional chemical system or the oxidation system. The conventional chemical disinfection system requires that the lenses soak in disinfecting solution for a minimum of four hours. Prior to lens insertion and after chemical disinfection, the lenses should be thoroughly rinsed with saline solution. The oxidation system uses a buffered form of hydrogen peroxide to sterilize the contact lenses. After soaking for the appropriate length of time in the hydrogen peroxide, the lenses are placed in a neutralizing solution so as to render the hydrogen peroxide non-irritating to the eye when inserted.

All methods of disinfection are effective if properly performed. Individual doctors usually have their own preferences for disinfection. Allergic reactions to certain chemicals used as preservatives may also influence the choice of systems.

In addition to daily cleaning and disinfection, a weekly cleaner has been developed by the contact lens solution manufacturers to remove protein deposits on soft contact lenses and to a lesser degree on gas permeable contact lenses. This cleaner is not used on hard contact lenses. As protein is a natural component of the tears, it often becomes bonded to the contact lenses. Daily cleaning does not always remove these deposits. The weekly cleaner is an enzyme which chemically breaks down the protein molecule and thus removes it from the surface of the contact lens. Weekly cleaning is performed after daily cleaning, but prior to sterilization.

Trouble Shooting Contact Lens Problems

Following are some common problems encountered by contact lens wearers, possible causes of the problems and their solutions. This material should be used for general informational purposes only and should not be used for specific self-diagnosis and treatment.

> ■ **Eye pain while wearing contact lenses**
> *causes include:* overwear of the lens, an excessively tight fitting lens, a foreign body under the lens, a damaged lens, a corneal abrasion or an infection. Other painful eye problems unassociated with contact lens wear may also be at fault.

recommended action: remove the lens, contact your ophthalmologist or other appropriate eye care professional for further instructions.

- **Eye pain after removal of contact lens**
  causes include: corneal abrasion, corneal edema, ischemic keratitis (irritation of cornea from poor oxygenation), contact lens overwear, foreign body, "tight lens syndrome", infection, other painful eye conditions unassociated with lens wear.

  recommended action: contact your ophthalmologist or other appropriate eye care professional for further instructions.

- **Variable or blurred vision with contact lenses**
  causes include: poorly fitting lens (too loose or too tight), wrong prescription, excessive tearing, mucus build-up on or under lens, damaged lens (torn or warped), poorly centered astigmatism lens.

  recommended action: thoroughly clean the lens (including enzyme with soft lenses), check the lens for obvious defects, consult your ophthalmologist or other appropriate eye care professional as necessary.

- **Blurred reading (or other close range) vision with contact lenses**
  causes include: presbyopia, other refractive problem, incorrect lens prescription.

  recommended action: consult your ophthalmologist or other appropriate eye care professional.

- **Lens rides up on eye with blink**
  causes include: loose fitting lens, damaged or warped lens, giant papillary conjunctivitis *(see page 139)*, other lid abnormalities.

  recommended action: consult your ophthalmologist or other appropriate eye care professional as necessary.

- **Burning sensation while wearing contact lens**
  causes include: allergy or irritation from lens solutions or contaminants, contact lens overwear, excessive use of eyes especially for close range work ("eye strain"), inadequate tear film ("dry eye syndrome")

recommended action: use non-preserved or "non-irritating" lens solutions, minimize use of eye make-up, thoroughly wash and rinse hands prior to handling lenses, remove lenses and substitute with glasses as necessary for excessive close work, use contact lens lubricating and rewetting solutions as necessary, contact ophthalmologist or other appropriate eye care professional as necessary for continued symptoms.

- **Itching**
Similar causes and recommendations as listed for "Burning" *(see above)*.
In addition, "giant papillary conjunctivitis" is a fairly common cause of itching, burning and general contact lens intolerance *(see page 139 for further information)*.

- **Redness of eyes while wearing contact lenses**
causes include: excessively tight fitting contact lens (redness tends to occur especially at the edges of the iris), allergy/intolerance to lens solutions, contact lens overwear, infection (usually associated with discharge).

recommended action: remove lens, contact ophthalmologist or other appropriate eye care professional.

- **Inability to remove contact lens**
causes include: "tight lens syndrome" (lens can tightly adhere to cornea leading to increased corneal edema and further tightening of lens), inexperience or improper technique of removal, incorrectly fit lens. It is also possible that lens has already fallen out of the eye or has slid up under the upper lid.

recommended action: ensure that the lens is still in the eye by direct inspection with a magnifying mirror or assistance from another observer. If the lens is definitely still in the eye, place a drop of rewetting solution, artificial tear or saline in the eye to "float" the lens on the cornea to aid removal. Occasionally, the lens rides up under the upper lid and becomes lodged here. *(Note: The lens can not slide "behind" the eye and become permanently lost.)* If it seems likely that the lens is under the upper lid due to foreign body sensation or "lens awareness", apply gentle pressure with a finger on the closed upper lid and look upward—this sometimes allows the lens to become "seated" on the cornea again where it can be removed; do not "sweep" under the lid with fingers or cotton tip applicators, etc. If not sure whether the lens is still in the eye, do not attempt removal as this may result in corneal abrasion or other serious eye injury. Consult your ophthalmologist or other appropriate eye care professional as necessary.

There are many other minor contact lens related problems that may arise which should be brought to the attention of your ophthalmologist or other eye care professional. When in doubt, communicate your problem to your doctor, do not attempt to self diagnose or treat. Very serious adverse consequences have been reported from such treatment including loss of eye sight in an infected eye.

Summary

Contact lenses are a very valuable, accepted means of vision correction. With proper care and handling, they can last up to two years in the case of soft contact lenses and for five years or more in the case of hard contact lenses and gas permeable lenses. To be successful at contact lens wear, one must never forget that contact lenses are foreign bodies on the eyes and, as such, require constant awareness of potential problems.

While proper care in cleaning and handling will reduce the possibility of problems, a close dialogue between patient and doctor is imperative to preserve good ocular health and clear vision for a lifetime.

CARE & MAINTENANCE

Low Vision Care

The prescription of conventional eyeglasses often fails to adequately improve the function of individuals who have very limited central vision (usually 20/100 or worse) due to macular degeneration, diabetic retinopathy, and other serious eye disorders. The physical damage to the eye in these conditions limits the potential visual acuity regardless of how well the eye is focused by correction of the refractive error (nearsightedness, farsightedness, astigmatism).

Patients in this category may be candidates for special "low - vision" devices such as magnifiers, telescopic lenses, prism glasses, etc. The measurement of visual function, selection of appropriate vision aids and the instruction in thier use constitute "low vision care". There are many nonoptical low vision aids available as well, including large print books, newspapers and periodicals, special time pieces, playing cards, telephone dialing aids, check writing guides, etc.

A team approach to low vision care utilizing the services of ophthalmologists, optometrists and opticians provides the best results.

Although considerable improvement may be possible with low vision aids, expectations must be tempered by the realistic understaning that nothing, in most cases, can correct the underlying physical damage to the macula or optic nerve. Low vision aids simply help the eyes to work more efficiently by enlarging images.

Patients with profound visual loss require more comprehensive rehabilitation programs. With Braille instruction, occupational training, guide dogs, and other special assistance many otherwise handicapped individuals can lead full and productive lives.

The interested reader is referred to the Resources and References Section in the appendix for further information.

MEDICAL TREATMENT

General Information

There are several issues relating to medical treatment in general that should be clarified prior to presenting specific information on medical eye care.

dose/response—all medications have a characteristic onset of action, peak effect and duration of action. These can be plotted out to form so-called "dose/response curves." Some medicines, for example, may begin to work almost immediately, reach peak effect in a half hour and wear off in an hour. This "behavior pattern" may necessitate frequent (hourly) usage of the medicine to maintain a therapeutic effect. Other medicines work much more slowly (e.g., "sustained release") and may only require once or twice a day usage.

The severity of the condition being treated also determines the frequency of usage of the medicine. The point is, when a medicine is prescribed for usage at certain intervals, it is for a good reason and it should not be used in some alternate random fashion.

generic vs. brand name medicines—all drugs and medicines have chemical names. Pharmaceutical companies usually add an easily pronounced and remembered "brand name" to their version of the drug. If they hold an exclusive patent for that medication, their brand name may be the only familiar designation for that medication until the patent expires.

When a pharmacist is authorized by the prescribing doctor to fill a prescription "generically" he can substitute another (usually less expensive) brand or chemical equivalent.

Ordinarily, the consumer can be assured that there is no significant difference in quality between brand name medicines and "generic equivalents".

allergies—allergies are hypersensitive reactions of the body's immune system to various substances in the environment (internal or external). An individual can have or develop allergies to almost anything including dusts, pollens, animal dander, various chemicals and drugs and even one's own body tissues. Drug allergies can occur by all routes of administration including pills, drops, injections, etc.

Some drug allergies are slight and insignificant; others may cause an acute anaphylactic reaction and sudden death by respiratory arrest.

It is important to distinguish allergic drug reactions from toxic or other types of reactions. Many patients will report an "allergy" to a certain drug or medicine when, in fact, they previously had some other type of untoward reaction which may simply have been a normal side effect of that medicine (see below).

The ophthalmologist is specially trained to distinguish between these different types of reaction and is careful to prescribe medicines accordingly and to recognize and appropriately treat any reactions that do occur.

side effects—most medicines have an intended main effect and one or more side effects which may range from inconsequential to severe. Some glaucoma eye drops, for example, are very effective at controlling the glaucoma but can also cause potentially serious breathing and heart problems in predisposed individuals. The ophthalmologist is specially trained in pharmacology and physiology to be able to anticipate and minimize such reactions by selecting the proper medications for each individual and appropriately adjusting the dosage.

drug interactions—there are many possible interactions (both beneficial and harmful) that can occur between different medicines that an individual is taking. It is important that a complete listing of all drugs and medicines be given to the treating ophthalmologist so that medication and dosage selection can be properly made.

medication toxicities—many medications can cause toxic or adverse reactions especially when used for long periods of time. The ophthalmologist is trained to monitor and recognize these reactions and to appropriately adjust or discontinue the medication as needed.

pregnancy—whenever possible no medications by any route should be administered to a pregnant woman especially during the first trimester. Many medications are known to cause fetal damage and many others may have undiscovered harmful potential. As always, the appropriate physicians should be consulted prior to any medication usage during pregnancy.

tolerance—when used for long periods of time some medications lose their effectiveness—the individual is said to have become tolerant to the medication and may either need a stronger dosage or a different medication to achieve the same intended effect. Only by regular examinations can it be determined whether an individual has become tolerant to his medication.

self-medication—it cannot be overemphasized that self diagnosis and treatment are potentially very dangerous. Ophthalmologists are continually faced with the patient who incorrectly administers prescription eye medication to himself or his family and causes serious damage and even blindness.

There are simply too many complexities in modern day pharmacology for an untrained lay person to be able to correctly administer medications. A detailed understanding of all the points mentioned above is only the beginning of a proper training. Years of clinical experience then help refine the skills and judgment required of a qualified eye physician.

prescription sharing—this is a common form of self medication. Parents, often mistakenly, will reason that the antibiotic eye drop prescribed for one child's eye infection will be appropriate for the brother or sister who comes down with a similar problem.

In some cases parents, hoping to prevent spread of infection, will treat unaffected family members with the antibiotic that was prescribed specifically for one individual. In the case of eye infections, this can result in spread of infection from the contaminated dropper bottle that would not otherwise have occurred.

labels—it is extremely important that labels on medications be read correctly and the instructions followed closely. The eye drop label contains the appropriate information regarding which eye is to be treated, for how long and the proper dosage and frequency of usage, etc. Additional information regarding refills, proper storage and warnings, etc. is also often listed on the label.

Medications are also assigned expiration dates beyond which the potency of the drug may be lost. The date is usually stamped on the container but may be obscured by the label or be difficult to interpret. The pharmacist or ophthalmologist should be consulted if their is any question about the expiration date and potency of the medication.

compliance—this is one of the more difficult issues relating to proper use of medications. The correct medicine may be prescribed and all the necessary labeling and instruction given but little or no benefit will be gained if the individual does not comply with the program.

It is, of course, often difficult with long term daily medicine use, to keep on a rigid, unfailing schedule. This is, however, the secret to success in the long term management of such chronic eye conditions as glaucoma, etc.

As you will note from the above, a great deal goes into the selection and prescription of eye medications and, unless directions are reliably followed, the full benefit of all this effort will not be realized.

The Use of Eye Medications

Following are some commonly asked questions regarding the use of eye medications:

What is the best way to use eye drops?

The illustration on the next page demonstrates one simple, safe and reliable method of using drops. Basically, the lower lid should be gently pulled away from the eye creating a small "pocket" or "pouch". The dropper bottle is then slowly brought into position just above the pocket and gently squeezed until one drop is felt in the eye. The hand holding the dropper bottle can rest on the cheek bone for steadiness and support. Eye ointments can be instilled in a similar fashion. Ordinarily a strip of ointment measuring one half to three quarters of the length of the lower lid should be used.

Some individuals find that the easiest way of instilling eye drops is while lying on their back in bed or resting their head backwards in a recliner chair.

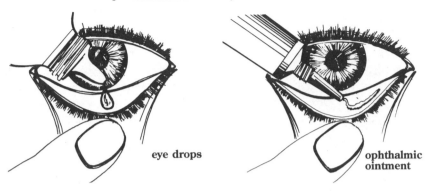

eye drops

ophthalmic
ointment

How do I know if the drop actually went in my eye?

Usually the drop can be felt as a cool sensation and some-times as a mild "stinging" or "burning" in the eye. If you simply feel the wetness on your lid or face you probably missed the eye. Refrigeration of the drops is a simple trick to allow for better awareness of the drop entering the eye.

What if I'm not sure that the drop went in? Can I repeat it?

Yes. When in doubt, there is no harm to repeating the drop once. The eye does not even hold more than a single drop at a time—the excess will simply drip or be blinked out. It is definite-ly better to repeat the drop unnecessarily rather than miss a scheduled dose.

Should I keep my eyes closed or do anything else after using eye drops?

Yes, ideally, the eyes should be kept gently closed for fifteen to thirty seconds to allow for absorption of the drop into the eyes. With some drops, particularly the beta blockers used for glaucoma *(see page 83)*, the bridge of the nose should be compressed for a minute or so to prevent drainage of the drop down the nasolacrimal duct *(see page 8)*. Drainage down the tear ducts can both lessen the effectiveness of the drops in the eyes and lead to absorption of the drop into the blood stream through the nasal capillaries. This, in turn, increases the risk of systemic

(general body) side effects from the drops. The illustration demonstrates the technique of nasal compression. Be sure not to just pinch the skin of the nose. The thumb and forefinger should press against the bony bridge in the area of the tear sacs.

Is it normal for eye drops to sting or burn after instillation?

Yes, many people will experience a transient burning or stinging sensation but this varies quite a bit from person to person and depends on the type and strength of drop being used.

I'm using several different types of glaucoma drops. Does it make a difference how close together I use them?

Ideally, the different drops should be used at staggered intervals of several hours to avoid dilution or washing out of one drop by another and to smooth out the "peaks and valleys" of medication effectiveness. If this is not practical, a few minutes delay between drops will at least decrease the dilution effect.

Is there some significance to the color of the dropper bottle caps?

Yes, red caps usually indicate that the drops are in class called "mydriatic/cycloplegics" which cause temporary dilation of the pupil and decreased accommodation (close range focus). Green caps indicate that the drops are "miotics" which constrict the pupil and lower intraocular pressure. Efforts are being made to further color code all classes of eye drops to help avoid errors in usage of the drops.

Does it make any difference how eye drops are stored?

Most eye drops can be kept at room temperature but some require refrigeration. This is usually specified on the label. As with all medications, care should be exercised to keep eye drops out of the reach of children. Expiration dates should be checked prior to reusing a stored eye drop.

What about the "over the counter" eye drops?

Most "OTC" products can be used safely provided the package insert is carefully read and understood. Artificial tears can be very safe and effective drops to soothe tired or dry eyes. Eye washes and baths must be used carefully to avoid injury to the eye from the cup or dispenser. Decongestant drops should not be overused. Persistent redness or irritation of the eyes should be reported to your ophthalmologist.

What do all those abbreviations mean on the doctor's prescription?
Here is a brief summary of some of the more commonly used abbreviations:

O.D= right eye	h.s. = at bedtime
O.S. = left eye	p.o. = orally
O.U. = both eyes	oph sol = ophthalmic solution
q.d. = once daily	oph ung = ophthalmic oint-ment
b.i.d. = twice daily	gtts = drops
t..i.d. = three times daily	ml = milliliter (measure of volume)
q.i.d. = four times daily	mg = milligram (measure of weight)

Any other tips on using eye drops?
Yes, prior to using, check, check and recheck the label. Inappropriate use of the wrong eye drops can cause severe damage to the eyes. There have also been many instances of ocular injury from the mistaken use of various household liquids including glues and adhesives!

It is especially important to check ointments and creams as there are many different types of medications and other substances that are supplied in tubes.

Also, don't self medicate or overmedicate. Always consult your ophthalmologist for the proper prescription of eye medications. Serious side effects commonly result from the prolonged inappropriate use of "cortisone" containing eye drops. These and many other types of eye medication should not be casually used as "eye washes" or "whiteners".

Commonly Used Eye Medications

Following is a roster of various classes of eye medications listing some common brand names, their manufacturers and major active ingredients. This listing is not intended to be encyclopedic and does not reflect any bias or preference for a particular medication or manufacturer. For further information on ophthalmic pharmaceuticals and available preparations, please consult your ophthalmologist or contact your local ophthalmology or medical society.

DECONGESTANTS	
"whiten" the eyes by constricting conjunctival capillaries—relieve minor, nonspecific eye irritations	
Common brand names	**Major active ingredient(s)**
Albalon® (Allergan)	naphazoline HCl 0.1%
Clear Eyes® (Ross)	naphazoline HCl 0.012%
Collyrium Eye Drops with Tetrahydrozoline® (Wyeth)	tetrahydrozoline HCl 0.05%
Comfort® Eye drops (Barnes Hind)	naphazoline HCl 0.03%
Murine® Plus (Ross)	tetrahydrozoline 0.05%
Naphcon® (Alcon)	naphazoline HCl 0.012%
Ocuclear Eye Drops® (Schering)	oxymetazoline HCl 0.025%
Prefrin™ (Allergan)	phenylephrine HCl 0.12%
Visine® (Leeming)	tetrahydrozoline HCl 0.05%
Vasocon® (IOLAB)	naphazoline HCl 0.1%
DECONGESTANTS WITH ANTIHISTAMINE	
"whiten" the eyes by constriction of conjunctival capillaries and help relieve the adverse effects (itching, burning, etc.) of histamine on the eye	
Albalon-A® (Allergan)	naphazoline HCl 0.05% antazoline phosphate 0.5%
Naphcon-A® (Alcon)	naphazoline HCl 0.025% pheniramine maleate 0.3%
Prefrin-A™ (Allergan)	phenylephrine HCl 0.12% pyrilamine maleate 0.1%
Vasocon-A® (IOLAB)	naphazoline HCl 0.05% antazoline phosphate 0.5%

ANTIBIOTICS /ANTIBACTERIALS
used in the treatment of bacterial infections

Common Brand Names	Major Active Ingredient(s)
Bleph-10® drops and ointment (Allergan)	sulfacetamide sodium 10%
Cetamide® drops (Alcon)	sulfacetamide sodium 10%
Chibroxin™ drops (Merk, Sharp & Dohme)	norfloxacin, MSD 0.03%
Ciloxan™ drops (Alcon)	ciprofloxacin HCl 0.3%
Chloroptic® drops and ointment (Allergan)	chloramphenicol (drops = 0.5%, ointment = 1.0%)
Erythromycin Ophthalmic Ointment (Pharmaderm)	erythromycin
Garamycin® drops and ointment (Schering)	gentamicin sulfate
Genoptic® drops and ointment (Allergan)	gentamicin sulfate
Gentacidin® drops and ointment (IOLAB)	gentamicin sulfate
Isoptocetamide® drops (Alcon)	sulfacetamide sodium 15%
Neosporin® drops (Burroughs Wellcome)	polymyxin B sulfate, neomycin sulfate, gramicidin
Neosporin® ointment (Burroughs Wellcome)	polymyxin B sulfate, bacitracin zinc, neomycin sulfate
Polysporin® ointment (Burroughs Wellcome)	polymyxin B, bacitracin
Polytrim® drops (Allergan)	trimethoprim sulfate, polymyxin B sulfate
Sodium Sulamyd® drops (Schering)	sulfacetamide sodium 10% & 30%
Sodium Sulamyd® ointment (Schering)	sulfacetamide sodium 10%
Sulf-10® drops (IOLAB)	sulfacetamide sodium 10%
Tobrex® drops and ointment (Alcon)	tobramycin 0.3%

CORTICOSTEROIDS
used in the treatment of various inflammatory conditions of the eyes and eyelids such as allergies, chemical irritations, uveitis, episcleritis, etc.

Common Brand Names	Major Active Ingredient(s)
Decadron® drops (Merck Sharp & Dohme)	dexamethasone sodium phosphate 0.1%
Decadron® ointment (Merck Sharp & Dohme)	dexamethasone sodium phopsphate 0.05%
Econopred® drops (Alcon)	prednisolone acetate 1/8% and 1.0%
Flarex® drops (Alcon)	flurometholone acetate 0.1%
Fluor-Op® drops (IOLAB)	flurometholone 0.1%
FML® drops and ointment (Allergan)	fluorometholone 0.1%
FML Forte® (Allergan)	fluorometholone 0.25%
HMS® drops (Allergan)	medrysone 1.0%
Inflamase® Mild drops (IOLAB)	prednisolone sodium phosphate 1/8%
Inflamase® Forte drops (IOLAB)	prednisolone sodium phosphate 1.0%
Maxidex® drops and ointment (Alcon)	dexamethasone
Pred Mild® drops (Allergan)	prednisolone acetate 0.12%
Pred Forte® drops (Allergan)	prednisolone acetate 1.0%

NON STEROIDAL ANTI-INFLAMMATORY AGENTS
used for certain inflammatory eye conditions

Acular® drops (Allergan)	ketorolac tromethamine 0.5%
Ocufen® drops (for use in eye surgery) (Allergan)	flurbiprofen 0.03%
Voltaren® drops (Ciba Vision Ophthalmics)	diclofenac 0.1%

ANTIBIOTIC/CORTICOSTEROID COMBINATIONS
used for treatment of certain conditions
with both infectious and inflammatory components
at the discretion of the prescribing physician

Common Brand Names	Major Active Ingredient(s)
Blephamide® drops and ointment (Allergan)	sulfacetamide sodium, prednisolone acetate
Cetapred® ointment (Alcon)	sulfacetamide sodium, prednisolone acetate
Cortisporin® drops (Burroughs Wellcome)	polymyxin B sulfate, neomycin sulfate, hydrocortisone
Cortisporin® ointment (Burroughs Wellcome)	polymyxin B sulfate, bacitracin zinc, neomycin sulfate, hydrocortisone
Dexacidin® drops and ointment (IOLAB)	neomycin and polymyxin B sulfates and dexamethasone
FML-S™ drops (Allergan)	flurometholone, sulfacetamide sodium
Isopto Cetapred® drops (Alcon)	sulfacetamide sodium, prednisolone acetate
Maxitrol® drops and ointment (Alcon)	neomycin and polymyxin B sulfates and dexamathasone
Metimyd® drops and ointment (Schering)	sulfacetamide sodium, prednisolone acetate
Neodecadron® drops and ointment (Merck, Sharp and Dohme)	neomycin sulfate, dexamethasone sodium phosphate
Ophthocort® ointment (Parke-Davis)	chloramphenicol, polymyxin B sulfate, hydrocortisone acetate
Poly-Pred® drops (Allergan)	neomycin sulfate, polymyxin B sulfate, prednisolone acetate
Pred-G™ drops (Allergan)	prednisolone acetate, gentamicin sulfate
Tobradex® drops and ointment (Alcon)	tobramycin, dexamethasone
Vasocidin® drops (IOLAB)	sulfacetamide sodium, prednisolone sodium phosphate
Vasocidin® ointment (IOLAB)	sulfacetamide sodium, prednisolone acetate

ANTIVIRALS
used in the treatment of herpes simplex ocular infections

Common Brand Names	Major Active Ingredient(s)
Herplex® drops (Allergan)	idoxuridine 0.1%
Stoxil® drops and ointment (Smith Kline French)	idoxuridine (drops = 0.1%, ointment = 0.5%)
Vira-A® ointment (Parke-Davis)	vidarabine 3%
Viroptic® drops (Burroughs Wellcome)	trifluridine 1%

GLAUCOMA MEDICATIONS
used in the management of glaucoma

MIOTICS
(constrict pupil as well as lower intraocular pressure)

Adsorbocarpine® drops (Alcon)	pilocarpine hydrochloride
Isopto Carbachol® drops (Alcon)	carbachol 0.75%, 1.5%, 2.25%, 1%, 2%, 4%, 3.0%
Isopto Carpine® drops (Alcon)	pilocarpine hydrochloride 0.25%, 0.5%, 1%, 2%, 3%, 4%, 5%, 6%, 8%, 10%
Pilagan™ drops (Allergan)	pilocarpine nitrate 1%, 2%, 4%
Pilocar® drops (IOLAB)	pilocarpine hydrochloride 0.5%, 1%, 2%, 3%, 4%, 6%
Pilopine HS® gel (Alcon)	pilocarpine hydrochloride 4%

INDIRECT ACTING MIOTICS

Floropryl® ointment (Merck, Sharp & Dohme)	isoflurophate 0.025%
Humorsol® drops (Merck, Sharp & Dohme)	demecarium bromide 0.125%, 0.25%
Phospholine Iodide® drops (Ayerst)	echothiophate iodide 0.03%, 0.06%, 0.125%, 0.25%

BETA BLOCKERS

Betagan® drops (Allergan)	levobunolol HCl 0.5%
Betoptic® drops (Alcon)	betaxolol HCl 0.5%
Betoptic® S drops (Alcon)	betaxolol HCl 0.25%
Ocupress® drops (Otsuka America Pharmaceutical)	carteolol HCl 0.1%
OptiPranolol™ drops (Bauch & Lomb)	metipranolol HCl 0.3%
Timoptic® drops (Merck, Sharp & Dohme)	timolol maleate 0.25%, 0.5%

EPINEPHRINE PREPARATIONS	
Common Brand Names	**Major Active Ingredient(s)**
Epifrin® drops (Allergan)	epinephrine 0.25%, 0.5%, 1%, 2%
Epinal® drops (Alcon)	epinephryl borate 0.5%, 1%
Eppy/N® drops (Barnes Hind)	epinephryl borate 0.5%, 1%, 2%
Glaucon® drops (Alcon)	epinephrine hydrochloride 1%, 2%
Propine® drops (Allergan)	dipivefrin HCl 0.1%

MYDRIATICS
dilate the pupils

Mydfrin® drops (Alcon)	phenylephrine HCl 2.5%
Neo-Synephrine® drops (Winthrop)	phenylephrine HCl 2.5%, 10%

MYDRIATIC/CYCLOPLEGICS
dilate the pupil and inhibit ciliary body function (focusing mechanism), reduce intraocular muscle spasm associated with inflammation

Atropine Sulfate® drops and ointment (Allergan)	atropine sulfate (drops = 1%, ointment = 0.5%, 1.0%)
Cyclogyl® drops (Alcon)	cyclopentolate HCl 0.5%, 1.0%, 2.0%
Cyclomydril® drops (Alcon)	cyclopentolate HCl 0.2%, phenylephrine HCl 1.0%
Isopto Atropine® drops (Alcon)	atropine sulfate 0.5%, 1%., 3%
Isopto Homatropine® drops (Alcon)	homatropine hydrobromide 2%, 5%
Isopto Hyoscine® drops (Alcon)	scopolamine hydrobromide 0.25%
Mydriacyl® drops (Alcon)	tropicamide 0.5%, 1.0%

HYPEROSMOTICS
reduce swelling of the cornea by drawing fluid out of the swollen tissues

Adsorbonac® drops (Alcon)	sodium chloride 2%, 5%
Muro 128® ointment (Bausch & Lomb)	sodium chloride 5%
Muro 128® drops (Bausch & Lomb)	sodium chloride 2%, 5%

Other Routes for Medical Treatment of Eye Disease

Although eye drops and ointments are most frequently used, there are a number of other means by which medical eye care is administered.

Oral medications

Carbonic Anhydrase Inhibitors

Some cases of glaucoma require the addition of oral medicine to the eye drop regimen. Classified as carbonic anhydrase inhibitors (CAI) , these medications work by reducing the amount of aqueous humor (internal fluid) produced within the eye thus lowering the intraocular pressure.

Acetazolamide (Diamox®, Lederle Laboratories) is the most commonly used member of this class and is supplied in both oral (125 mg tablets, 250 mg tablets, 500 mg sustained release sequels®) and injectable (IV) forms.

Short term therapy with acetazolamide is usually well tolerated but may produce minor side effects such as tingling ("pins and needles") sensation in the hands and feet and occasional drowsiness and lethargy. Loss of appetite may also occur. Excessive urination commonly results from the diuretic ("water pill") effect of acetazolamide.

Long term therapy may rarely be associated with more serious side effects including potassium depletion, kidney stones and anemia. Care must be exercised by the ophthalmologist and internist to monitor for and treat any of these complications. Potassium replacement in the form of fruit juices, bananas or pills is often recommended as an adjunct to long term acetazolamide therapy especially when other diuretics are being used.

Methazolamide (Neptazane®, Lederle Laboratories, 25 mg and 50 mg tablets) is another member of the CAI class and can be used as an alternative to acetazolamide.

Corticosteroids

Cortisone derivatives or corticosteroids (prednisone, methylprednisolone, etc.) are often used by ophthalmologists for some serious ocular inflammatory conditions. Prednisone is most commonly used and can be given orally, intravenously, and by periocular injection (next to the eye). Short term oral prednisone therapy is usually well tolerated but side effects tend to develop with increasing dosages and durations of treatment. Stomach irritation, elevated blood pressure and blood sugar, bone, muscle and skin problems, as well as nervous system and emotional complications can all occur with prolonged use. Cataracts and glaucoma can also develop as a result of long term prednisone therapy.

The body's normal production of cortisone (a life sustaining hormone), is suppressed by administration of prednisone and caution must be exercised when discontinuing long term treatment so that a severe and even life threatening reaction does not occur. Treatment is usually slowly tapered so that the body can resume its normal cortisone production on its own. Many doctors use an "alternate-day" regimen for long term high dose prednisone treatment to lessen the chance of complications from chronic use. The ophthalmologist will often consult with an internist when maintaining a patient on long term steroid therapy.

Anti-infectives

Anti-infectives include a vast array of antibiotics for bacterial infections, and antivirals and antifungals for certain viral and fungal infections. Many ocular infections can be adequately treated with topical (drop or ointment) preparations but more severe internal ocular or orbital infections require oral or even IV anti-infective medication.

A careful microbiologic work-up is usually performed and the most appropriate anti-infective is prescribed. Indiscriminate use of antibiotics for routine eye infections is discouraged. The ophthalmologist and sometimes an infectious disease expert should be consulted for treatment of this kind.

Others

Oral pain medications sometimes become necessary for painful eye injuries and inflammations and should always be used exactly according to the ophthalmologist's instructions. Serious side effects and even dependencies can develop from the improper use of the more potent pain medications.

Less commonly used oral medications for eye disease include some chemotherapeutic agents for severe inflammations and nonsteroidal anti-inflammatory drugs (NSAIDs) such as indomethacin for certain ocular inflammatory disorders.

Injectable medications

In addition to topical and oral routes, injection of medicines is sometimes necessitated. Injection can be intravenous.(IV), intramuscular (IM) periocular or intraocular. The nature and severity of the condition dictate the preferred means of administration.

Periocular injection involves the placement of solutions (usually antibiotics or steroids) in close proximity to the eye. This is accomplished using a tiny needle that passes through the space between the eye and the lid. The injection is usually not painful and can be made easily tolerable by the prior administration of a topical anesthetic drop. Periocular injections are routinely performed at the conclusion of many eye operations including cataract surgery. Intraocular injections (within the eye) are usually only performed for severe, vision threatening eye infections *(see endophthalmitis, page 151)*.

Anesthetic solutions are also commonly injected in locations around the eyes and lids in preparation for eye surgery.

IV and less commonly IM injections are sometimes used for anti-infectives , steroids, CAIs *(see page 85)* or pain medications.

The intravenous administration of agents such as fluorescein *(see page 39)*, radiopaque dyes and tensilon, etc. is for diagnostic rather than therapeutic purposes.

Other Forms of Ophthalmic Treatment

Bandage Contact Lenses

A special type of soft contact lens can be used to treat various disorders of the cornea. Corneal edema, delayed healing of the corneal epithelium, recurrent corneal erosions, certain lid abnormalities, etc. are some of the conditions that may warrant the use of a bandage lens. These lenses can be worn around the clock but require careful monitoring by the ophthalmologist.

Collagen Corneal Shields

These contact lens-like devices made of collagen can be used for many of the same indications as the bandage soft lenses providing very effective support for healing of the cornea. The shield usually dissolves spontaneously in a few days.

Ocular Inserts

Punctum plugs are tiny plastic devices that can be temporarily inserted in the tear drainage pores (puncta) to help treat severe dry eye states *(see page 147)*.

Lacriserts® (Merck, Sharp & Dohme)are tiny rods that are placed inside the lower lids providing moisture as they slowly dissolve for the treatment of dry eyes .

Occuserts® (Alza) are very thin membranes impregnated with medication which can be inserted between the lower lid and the eyeball. The medicine is slowly and continually released over the span of a week at which time a new membrane is inserted by the patient.

SURGICAL TREATMENT

Surgical treatment of eye disease is usually reserved for situations where optical and medical treatment have failed or are inappropriate for the nature of the condition. Surgery involves the use of instruments or lasers to physically alter tissue in an effort to cure or correct an abnormality. Surgical eye treatment can only be performed by a qualified ophthalmologist. Some eye lid operations, however, are also performed by surgeons in other specialties.

The indications for eye surgery are usually considered on an individual basis. The ophthalmologist evaluates the situation and considers the relative risks and benefits of surgical intervention. The salient points should then be communicated to the patient and family for a valid informed consent.

No surgical procedure is one hundred percent successful one hundred percent of the time. Rapid advances in technology, however, have made most eye operations much more predictably successful when performed with discretion, judgment and skill. Long hospital stays are also largely a thing of the past with most eye surgery now being performed on an out-patient basis under "local anesthesia".

Local anesthesia involves the use of lidocaine, bupivicaine or similar anesthetic agent. Anesthetics are never injected into the eye but rather into the tissues surrounding the eye using very tiny needles which cause little, if any, real pain. Diffusion of the anesthetic then occurs effectively eliminating pain or undesirable eye movements. Depending on the needs of the individual patient, supplemental oral and/or IV sedation are also used for some "local" procedures.

General anesthesia using inhaled gases is reserved for some of the more involved major eye operations and in instances where local anesthesia is impossible, e.g., children and uncooperative patients.

Following are capsule summaries of the more commonly performed ocular surgical procedures with accompanying drawings to illustrate the major points of the operations:

Operations on the Eyes

Pterygium Excision *(see page 188 for full description of pterygium)*

A very precise tiny scalpel (either surgical steel or gemstone) is used to separate the pterygium from the underlying clear corneal tissue. The remainder of the pterygium is then trimmed from the conjunctiva. Small caliber absorbable sutures may then be used to properly close the tissue layers. Antibiotic ointment and a light patch are then usually applied.

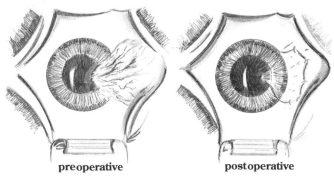

preoperative   postoperative

Eye drops are then used for two weeks or so and complete healing can be expected within three or four weeks. Complications such as infection are extremely rare. Recurrences of the pterygium can, and do, occur.

Corneal Transplantation (Penetrating Keratoplasty)

The specific indications for corneal transplant surgery are multiple and technically complex. Basically, when vision is failing due to any of a number of corneal disorders or when the integrity of the cornea is disrupted (some severe infections and inflammations or injuries) a transplant may be indicated.

"new" clear donor cornea

diseased cloudy cornea

A portion of full thickness cornea is carefully removed using an ultraprecise corneal trephine. A similar sized "button" is then removed form a donor cornea and sutured to the edges of the "host" cornea.

The corneal transplant procedure may be combined with other operations including cataract extraction with intraocular lens implantation ("triple procedure").

Postoperative care involves long term use of eye drops and a number of follow-up visits to the ophthalmologist. The results of corneal transplant surgery vary greatly depending on the circumstances requiring the operation, the health of the patient and the quality of the donor cornea.

REFRACTIVE CORNEAL SURGERY (KERATOREFRACTIVE SURGERY)

This is actually a group of surgical procedures aimed at reducing or eliminating the various refractive errors (nearsightedness, farsightedness and astigmatism). Refractive procedures include radial keratotomy, keratomileusis, lamellar refractive keratoplasty and various other incisions and resections of the cornea as well as newer laser "scupting" of the cornea.

This is a rapidly evolving area within ophthalmology which will soon benefit from sophisticated laser technologies.

*Coverage here is limited to **radial keratotomy (RK)** and **photorefractive keratoplasty (PRK)**. The reader is advised to consult his or her ophthalmologist for further details on these and other refractive procedures.*

Photorefractive Keratoplasty (PRK)

This is a new procedure currently in the final stages of FDA approval in the U.S. It is being performed more and more widely elsewhere in the world. Laser light, most commonly produced by the excimer laser, is used to reshape the cornea and thereby reduce near-

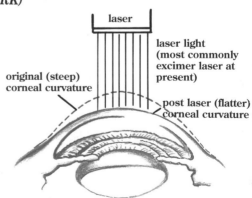

laser

laser light (most commonly excimer laser at present)

original (steep) corneal curvature

post laser (flatter) corneal curvature

sightedness. This procedure is expected to become a major means of refractive error correction in this country in the near future. Improvements in post-laser corneal healing and clearing and refinements to allow for correction of astigmatism and far-sightedness will expand the scope and utility of this technique.

Radial Keratotomy (RK)

First developed in the 1970s on a large scale, radial keratotomy is still evolving as techniques and instrumentation improve and data from new studies are accumulated.

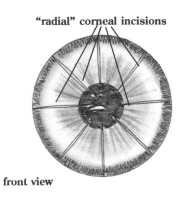

"radial" corneal incisions

front view

The purpose of the procedure is to reduce or eliminate nearsightedness (myopia) by flattening the corneal curvature. This is achieved by making several radial (spoke-like) partial thickness incisions in the corneal periphery. The "optical center" of the cornea is spared allowing for clear passage of light rays.

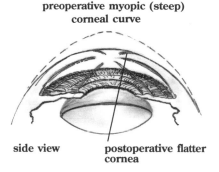

preoperative myopic (steep) corneal curve

side view　　**postoperative flatter cornea**

The exact number, location and depth of the incisions is determined by the degree of myopia and the individual surgeon's preference. Very high degrees of myopia are not as amenable to RK as are the lesser degrees. The procedure is ordinarily performed under local anesthesia on an outpatient basis. Careful preoperative ultrasonic measurements are routinely performed.

Complications, though rare, can occur. Over and under corrections and fluctuating vision are also possible. Despite some minor shortcomings of the present techniques, there is no disputing that RK has allowed millions of individuals to see clearly without glasses or contact lenses and is becoming more and more popular and accepted.

Astigmatism and **farsightedness** can also be corrected within certain limitations by variations in keratotomy techniques.

Cataract Extraction *(see page 132 for a full discussion of cataracts)*

The specific indications for cataract surgery vary quite a bit from surgeon to surgeon. The most commonly accepted approach is to consider surgery when the individual is having significant difficulty in his or her day-to-day existence due to vision loss from the cataract.

In the vast majority of cases the surgery is performed under local anesthesia in an "out-patient" setting. Extracapsular surgery either by "phacoemulsification" or "nuclear expression" is the preferred method. In *neither* case, contrary to popular belief, is laser energy used, though this may change in the near future.

By either method the bulk of the "capsule" (envelope)of the human lens is preserved and left in the eye. This maintains the integrity of the inner eye and has greatly reduced the rate of complications from cataract surgery.

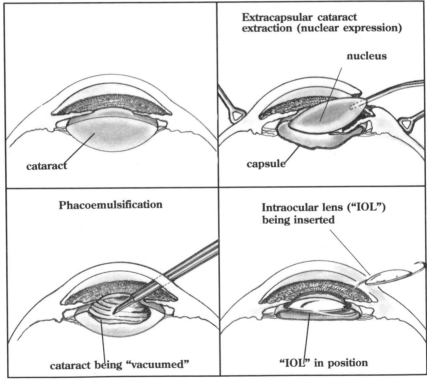

Cataract/implant surgery

In most cases an intraocular lens (IOL) is inserted into the "capsular bag". This restores the focus power normally supplied by the human lens. In rare instances an IOL cannot be used and either a contact lens or cataract glasses are needed to restore vision after the operation. Newer multifocal and soft, foldable IOL's are constantly evolving.

Postoperative care involves the use of eye drops for a few weeks and periodic check-ups by the ophthalmologist. Depending on the exact method used for the surgery, activities are restricted somewhat for a variable period of time. After phacoemulsification most activities can be resumed almost immediately. Full incision nuclear expression surgery requires restricted lifting and straining for a few weeks.

IOLs can also be inserted in the eyes of select patients who have previously undergone cataract extraction *without* an implant even years after the original operation. Consult your ophthalmologist for details regarding secondary intraocular lens implantation. Newer techniques including single stitch and even no-stitch incisions are currently evolving.

Glaucoma Filtering Surgery

When medications and laser treatments have failed to adequately control a case of glaucoma *(see page 163)*, surgery may be indicated to lower the intraocular pressure. A tiny opening is made in the sclera ("white" of the eye) which allows for drainage (filtration) of the intraocular fluid (aqueous) into the space between the sclera and the overlying conjunctiva ("skin" of the eye). A small bleb ("filtering bleb") is thus formed. A number of procedures have been developed to this end and are called collectively "filtering procedures".

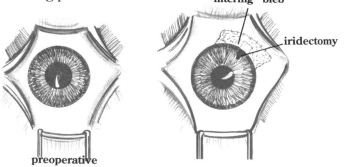

filtering "bleb"

iridectomy

preoperative

The most commonly performed filtering procedure is called "trabeculectomy". In this procedure a small flap of partial thickness sclera is first made under which the filtration opening ("ostium") is made. This produces a more controlled form of filtration. Special "antimetabolite" solutions are sometimes used to aid filtration.

Postoperative care involves the daily use of eye drops for a few weeks and close monitoring by the ophthalmologist. Both excessive and inadequate filtration can occur requiring special management and occasionally repeat procedures.

Newer laser procedures are being developed to accomplish the same result in a less invasive fashion.

Retinal Cryopexy

Certain types of retinal breaks (holes and tears) and degenerations require freezing of the surrounding retina to prevent development of a retinal detachment.

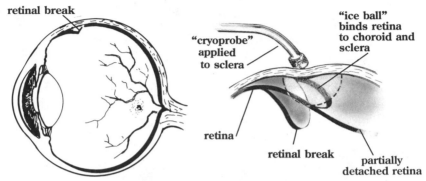

Using a special type of ophthalmoscope *(see indirect ophthalmoscopy, page 36)* and a freezing probe the area is localized and frozen. An adhesion (scar tissue connection) then develops between the retina and the underlying tissues which prevents separation (detachment) of the retina from the inside of the eye.

Drops are usually used for several days during which time activity is restricted and one or two postoperative check-ups are necessary to ensure that the retina is in place.

Retinal Detachment Repair

The most common type of retinal detachment *(rhegmatogenous retinal detachment—see page 193)* develops from a break (hole or tear) in the retina. In the early stages these breaks can be sealed by laser or cryoretinopexy. Once fluid has accumulated under the retina, a more involved procedure becomes necessary. The conventional means of repairing a retinal detachment is called a scleral buckling procedure.

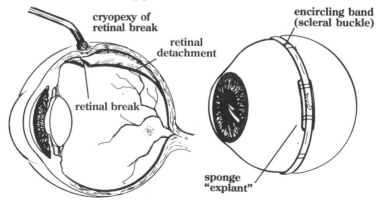

This procedure involves localization and treatment of the retinal break or breaks and the suturing of an elastic silicone sponge to the sclera in the area of the detachment. Drainage of subretinal fluid and the placement of an encircling band around the circumference of the eye may also be necessitated depending on the extent of the detachment. The purpose of the buckle is to indent the sclera so that it can contact and adhere to the detached retina. The adhesion is promoted by cryo or diathermy applications to the sclera.

Newer procedures have been developed to achieve the same result using tiny inflatable balloons on the surface of the eye or intraocular gas injections.

The surgery may be performed under local or general anesthesia depending on the age of the patient and the type and extent of detachment and the procedure being employed.

Postoperative care involves limitation of physical activities for a variable period of time and regular follow up exams to ensure that the retina remains attached.

Traction retinal detachments from intraocular scar tissue (diabetic retinopathy, etc.) require more extensive surgical procedures including scleral buckling and vitrectomy.

Vitrectomy

The term vitrectomy refers to the removal of vitreous humor from the eye. This may be performed from the front of the eye (anterior vitrectomy) usually in relatively small quantities or from the core of the vitreous (posterior vitrectomy). Occasionally, a partial vitrectomy is necessitated in the course of other types of eye operations (e.g., cataract surgery) when the vitreous presents in the surgical field or otherwise hinders or complicates the operation.

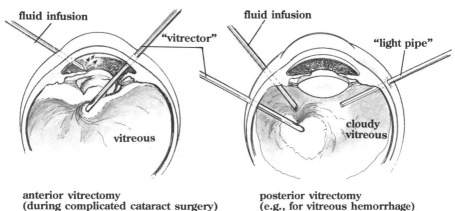

fluid infusion   **"vitrector"**   **fluid infusion**   **"light pipe"**

vitreous   **cloudy vitreous**

anterior vitrectomy
(during complicated cataract surgery)

posterior vitrectomy
(e.g., for vitreous hemorrhage)

Extensive posterior vitrectomies are reserved for such conditions as persistent vitreous hemorrhage *(see page 206)*, vitreous scar tissue, proliferative vitreoretinopathy *(see page 187)*, some cases of endophthalmitis *(see page 151)* and certain types of eye injuries.

Using very sophisticated microsurgical techniques, various tiny instruments can be introduced into the eye (irrigation/aspiration handpiece, microscissors and cutters, "light pipe", etc.) to perform the vitrectomy.

Depending on the specific condition being treated, various vitreous replacement substances may be used.

Results vary greatly with the condition being treated and cannot be generalized.

Strabismus Surgery *(Extraocular Muscle Surgery)*

When nonsurgical means (glasses, patching, exercises, etc.) have failed to adequately control a significant misalignment of the eyes, eye muscle surgery may be indicated.

This is usually performed under general anesthesia but on an out-patient basis. A great number of procedures have been devised and most surgeons develop their particular preferences and specialized techniques.

recession   resection

The most commonly performed procedures are *recessions* and *resections* of the horizontal rectus muscles. These muscles are ordinarily responsible for moving the eyes from "side to side".

A recession weakens the action of a muscle by moving it further toward the back of the eye. A resection strengthens the action of a muscle by shortening it. The amount of the recession or resection is dependent on the degree of misalignment of the eyes and requires that meticulous preoperative measurements be made by the ophthalmologist.

Though highly technically advanced, eye muscle surgery does not enjoy the same degree of predictability as some other eye operations. Additional procedures may be necessary for over- or undercorrections. Postoperative care usually involves the use of antibotic/steroid drops or ointment and regular follow-up appointments.

LASER EYE OPERATIONS

Lasers are simply very finely focused beams of uniform wavelength (color) light that can be used to treat many different tissues in the body including the eyes. The term laser is an acronym derived from Light Amplification by Stimulated Emission of Radiation.

The two basic types of lasers are "hot lasers" which treat by **photocoagulation** *(tissue heating) and "cold lasers" which treat by* **photodisruption** *(tissue vaporization). Lasers are further classified according to the wavelength (color) of light emitted. Some colors are more effective in treating certain ocular tissues than others.*

Laser operations are generally performed in the office or hospital out-patient setting and do not require the same elaborate preparation and sterile technique that conventional surgical procedures require.

Though lasers are widely used today in ophthalmic surgery, they can not be used for all procedures. Constantly evolving technology is, however, enlarging the spectrum of disorders that can be safely and effectively managed with this modality.

Following is a listing of some of the more commonly performed laser eye operations.

Argon Laser Trabeculoplasty (ALT)

This is a procedure for the treatment of open angle glaucoma *(see page 164)*. When medical treatment fails to adequately control the glaucoma, ALT can be quite effective in lowering the intraocular pressure.

A series of argon laser applications (from 50 to 100 coagulations) is made to the drainage meshwork within the eye. This most often results in an improved outflow of fluid from the eye which may last for years and lessen or even eliminate dependence on medications. The treatment can be extended or repeated but, in some cases, may be insufficient to control the pressure and filtering surgery becomes necessary *(see page 93)*.

Postoperative care involves the use of eye drops and close monitoring by the ophthalmologist to assess effectiveness of the procedure.

Peripheral Iridotomy (PI)

This is a procedure for the treatment of narrow angle and angle closure glaucoma *(see page 164)*. In these conditions there is often a build-up of pressure behind the iris tending to push it forward. By creating a tiny opening in the iris, aqueous fluid can flow freely forward thus equalizing the pressure on either side of the iris and preventing it from blocking the drainage meshwork of the eye.

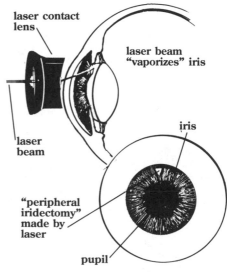

This can be accomplished with either the "hot" argon laser or the "cold" Nd YAG (neodymium Yttrium Aluminum Garnet) laser. Complications are less frequent with lasers as compared to the older conventional surgical techniques for PI which are still in use in special circumstances.

Postoperative care involves the use of eye drops and periodic follow-up exams by the ophthalmologist to ensure adequacy of the iris opening and control of the intraocular pressure.

YAG Laser Posterior Capsulotomy

In modern day extracapsular cataract surgery, a portion of the lens capsule is left in place to maintain the normal anatomic spaces of the eye and to serve as a support for the intraocular lens. In up to a third of cases this membrane develops a haziness which can cause symptoms similar to the original cataract.

Until recently this develop-

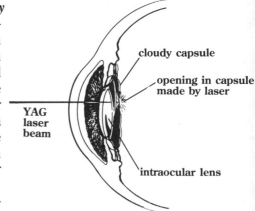

98

ment necessitated a surgical procedure to create an opening in the cloudy membrane. Now, however, this can be accomplished with the YAG laser in a short painless treatment often performed right in the office.

Using a Helium Neon (HeNe) aiming laser, the YAG energy can be critically focused on the opacified membrane. A few pulses are usually sufficient to create an opening that can restore clear vision without the need for conventional surgical incisions and their related potential complications.

Postoperative care involves the use of eyedrops and careful monitoring by the ophthalmologist to detect the occasional case of secondary glaucoma or retinal detachment that can ensue.

Retinal Photocoagulation

Various photocoagulating lasers (argon, krypton, tunable dye) can be used for the treatment of blood vessel disorders of the retina including diabetic retinopathy, vein occlusions and exudative macular degeneration. Lasers, in these cases, help to obliterate or seal abnormal blood vessels.

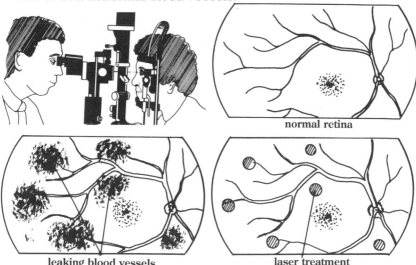

normal retina

leaking blood vessels   laser treatment

Treatment is usually conducted in an office setting or in a hospital out-patient department. A special contact lens is used to focus on the part of the retina being treated.

The results of retinal photocoagulation depend on the status of the eye being treated. In some cases, dramatic improvements in vision can be achieved; in others, treatment may be ineffectual due to the advanced and progressive nature of the disease.

Postoperative care usually involves the use of drops for a brief period of time and regular follow-up checks to monitor the status of the eye.

Laser Retinopexy

Retinal breaks *(holes and tears—see page 191)* can often be treated by laser. Providing certain criteria are met with regard to size, type and location of the break, laser treatment can seal the break preventing retinal detachment.

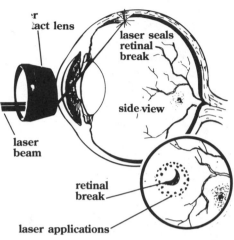

A special mirrored contact lens is used to visualize the break and to direct the laser beam (usually argon). Two or more rows of coagulations are placed around the break. The resultant adhesions that develop between the surrounding retina and the underlying tissues safeguard against detachment by preventing the seepage of fluid through the break and under the retina.

Despite adequate treatment, it is still possible to develop a retinal detachment from the original break or an additional new break.

Postoperative care includes limitation of activities for a variable period of time and careful follow-up checks by the ophthalmologist.

Photorefractive Keratoplasty (See Page 90)

Operations on the Lids and Lacrimal System

Chalazion (Incision And Drainage)

When an acutely infected chalazion *(see page 136)* fails to respond to medical treatment, incision and drainage can provide prompt relief.

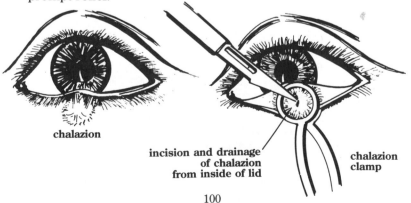

chalazion

incision and drainage
of chalazion
from inside of lid

chalazion
clamp

After suitable local anesthesia the eyelid is everted and a small vertical incision is made on the inside of the lid through which the contents of the chalazion are drained. This is ordinarily not painful and requires no sutures. The only outwardly visible sign of the procedure may be a small amount of swelling and bruising of the lid which disappears in a few days.

The eye is usually patched for a few hours to limit swelling and prevent bleeding and drops or ointment are applied for several days. Chalazions can recur in the same or adjacent locations.

Ptosis Repair

Ptosis (or blepharoptosis) is the term usually used to describe a drooping of the upper lid *(see page 189)*. This must be differentiated from "baggy eyelids" due to excessive skin laxity *(dermatochalasis, see page 143)* often seen in the elderly and in many others as a hereditary trait. Ptosis can involve the lids of one or both eyes.

In some cases, the ptosis is due to a neurologic condition and improves spontaneously as the underlying condition improves or is treated. In cases where the ptosis is permanent and is causing a significant *visual* impairment (limitation of upward peripheral vision) or a significant *cosmetic* impairment an operation can be performed to repair the ptosis.

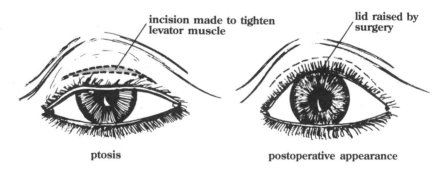

incision made to tighten levator muscle

lid raised by surgery

ptosis   postoperative appearance

There are many different surgical procedures for ptosis. The type and degree of ptosis as well as the surgeon's preference determine the selection of procedures. Surgery is usually performed on an outpatient basis and may require local or general anesthesia depending on the age of the patient and the type of procedure.

Ectropion Repair

An ectropion *(see page 150)* is an *outward* rotation of the lower eyelid (rarely of the upper lid). If the ectropion is causing excessive tearing, irritation of the eye or a significant cosmetic defect, surgical repair may be undertaken.

ectropion
(lid turned outward)

postoperative appearance
(lid in normal position)

This is usually performed under local anesthesia on an outpatient basis. Depending on the type and extent of the ectropion any of a number of surgical procedures may be appropriate. Ordinarily the lower lid is "shortened" by special plastic surgical techniques so that it lies tightly against the eye.

Postoperative care usually involves patching of the eye for one day to limit swelling and regular instillation of ophthalmic ointments for several days. Depending on the type of procedure performed, sutures may need to be removed within the first week or so postoperatively.

Entropion Repair

An entropion *(see page 152)* is an *inward* rotation of the lower eyelid (rarely of the upper lid). if the entropion is causing irritation of the eye, surgical repair may be undertaken.

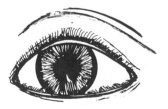

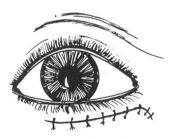

entropion
(lid/lashes turned
inward)

postoperative appearance
(lid in normal position)

This is usually performed under local anesthesia on an outpatient basis. Depending on the type and extent of the entropion, any of a number of surgical procedures may be appropriate. Using plastic surgical techniques, the lower lid margin is rotated outward from the eye to prevent the lashes from causing irritation to the cornea.

Postoperative care usually involves patching of the eye for one day to limit swelling and regular instillation of ophthalmic ointments for several days. Depending on the type of procedure performed, sutures may need to be removed within the first week or so postoperatively.

Blepharoplasty

Excess, redundant skin of the eyelids commonly develops with age but may be seen in much younger individuals on a hereditary basis *(see blepharochalasis and dermatochalasis pages 130 and 143).*

(see blepharochalasis and dermatochalasis pages 130 and 143)

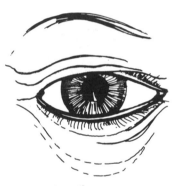

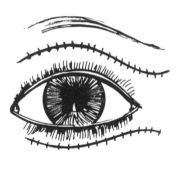

preoperative appearance   postoperative appearance

When a significant cosmetic defect results or when the excess skin is interfering with peripheral vision, surgical correction may be undertaken.

In some instances, the upper or lower lids alone are repaired; in other cases upper and lower lids of both eyes may require surgery.

Blepharoplasty is usually performed under local anesthesia on an outpatient basis. Excess skin is excised and, where indicated, protruding fatty tissue is also removed. Sutures are used to close the skin incisions and are usually removed within the first postoperative week.

Depending on surgeon preference, eye patches may or may not be used. Ordinarily there is a substantial degree of lid swelling and bruising which improves in two to three weeks.

CARE & MAINTENANCE

Probing and Irrigation of the Tear Ducts

Some infants are born with blocked tear ducts *(see page 131)*. If the blockage does not spontaneously improve, a probing and irrigation of the tear drainage system may be necessary.

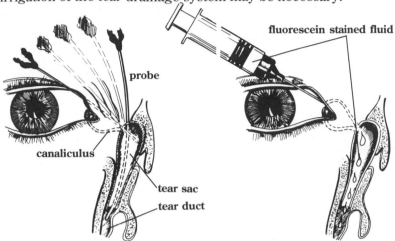

This is ordinarily performed in the hospital on an outpatient basis under brief general anesthesia. A small, blunt tipped wire probe is passed down the tear ducts to disrupt the blockage and a colored fluid is then irrigated through the system. If the fluid is recovered by gentle suction through the nose, patency of the tear drainage system is confirmed.

Occasionally, additional probings are necessary to achieve a permanent result. Probing and irrigation for blocked tear ducts in adults is usually not successful since the blockage is on a different basis and may require a DCR procedure (see below) if severe.

Dacryocystorhinostomy (DCR)

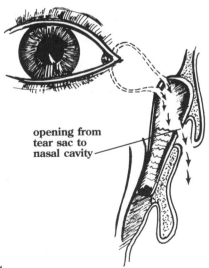

In cases of severe blockage of the tear drainage system often with recurrent tear sac infections, a DCR may be undertaken to establish a new connection between the tear ducts and the nasal passages.

Depending on the age of the patient and the severity of the condition, this procedure may be performed under local or general anesthesia. A tiny opening is made in the nasal bone through which the contents of the tear sac can empty into the nasal passages, reestablishing normal tear drainage.

Postoperative care involves eventual removal of sutures and any temporary nasal tubes and packing. Revisions and reoperations are sometimes necessary.

Miscellaneous

Enucleation

In some severe, end-stage ocular conditions when there is complete blindness in an eye which is painful or disfiguring, removal of the eye (enucleation) may be necessary. Other indications for enucleation include certain malignant ocular tumors, and some cases of severe ocular trauma.

A plastic sphere is implanted in the orbit (socket) in place of the eyeball and a prosthetic (artificial) eye shell is fabricated and custom fitted for the best cosmetic results.

Surgical management of lid and orbit abnormalities following enucleation may be necessary. Special care of the prosthesis and the socket is taught to the patient on an individual basis.

Evisceration is a partial enucleation wherein the scleral shell (white of the eye) is left intact while the intraocular contents are removed.

Exenteration is a much more extensive procedure involving removal of the entire orbital contents including the eye, extraocular muscles, orbital fat, and lids in cases of extremely malignant, invasive orbital tumors.

Remarkably, plastic and prosthetic surgery can often restore an acceptable cosmetic appearance.

OTHER FORMS OF EYE CARE

Eye Exercises and Vision Training

In modern ophthalmology, eye exercise programs are limited to orthoptic exercises to improve fusion (high level cooperation between the eyes) in some cases of eye muscle imbalance, especially convergence insufficiency *(see page 139)*, and to enhance the results of strabismus surgery.

There is no universally agreed upon data to show that special vision training or eye exercise programs are appropriate for the treatment of learning and reading disabilities or for the enhancement of visual acuity.

Patching (Occlusion) Therapy

Most cases of amblyopia *(see page 126)* in children under age eight or nine can be effectively treated by patching or occlusion of the stronger eye. This forces the weaker, amblyopic eye to be used exclusively during the time that the fellow eye is patched. Studies have shown that this treatment actually improves the transmission of visual impulses from the eye to the brain.

The duration and extent of patching are determined by the nature and severity of the amblyopia. Generally, patching is initially carried out daily during all waking hours and is tapered as the amblyopia improves. Infants and very young children must be seen at frequent intervals to ensure that amblyopia ("occlusion amblyopia") is not developing in the patched eye.

Form-fitting, flesh colored, self-adhesive bandages are available for this use (e.g., Opticlude®, Coverlet®). If the patches cause skin irritation, mild ophthalmic cortisone creams are sometimes used under the ophthalmologist's direction taking care to avoid contact with the eye.

Most children cooperate with patching programs but usually require gentle but firm support and encouragement during the early phases.

Nutrition Therapy

Research is currently being conducted regarding the potential visual benefits of dietary manipulation and nutritional supplements. To date, no definite recommendations can be made in this regard.

EMERGENCY TREATMENT

What constitutes an eye emergency?

It is important to first determine what is and what is not a true ocular emergency. Any of the following should prompt an emergency call to an ophthalmologist or other appropriate emergency medical facility:

- *sudden loss of vision or sudden blurred vision* (may be partial, i.e., "half vision", "gray-outs", etc. or complete and may occur in one or both eyes with or without accompanying pain and other symptoms)—*see page 126.*

- *sudden onset of double vision*—*see page 146* (perception of two objects where there should only be one—if of brief duration, does not usually constitute an emergency)

- *"flashes"* or *"flashes and floaters"*—*see pages 178, 192, 193 and 205* (perception of flashing or sparkling lights with or without "spots", "specks", "flies", or "cobwebs", etc.)

- *sudden marked distortion of vision* (objects may appear "elongated" , "stretched" or "twisted", etc.—usually of significance in individuals with exudative macular degeneration—*see page 175*).

- *severe redness of the eye(s)*with or without discharge, pain or visual symptoms

- *severe pain in the eye(s)*of sudden or gradual onset with or without visual symptoms or redness of the eye(s)

- *any non-trivial injury to the eye(s)*

There are other rare instances of true ocular emergency. When in doubt, call and discuss the situation with an ophthalmologist who will be able to determine by careful questioning whether a true emergency exists or not. Please also refer to page 27 for a listing of additional signs and symptoms that do not ordinarily constitute an emergency.

What to do in case of an eye emergency.

As in all emergency situations, it is important to remain calm and to carefully note the circumstances such as time of onset of symptoms, whether one or both eyes are involved, any other associated symptoms, activities involved in at time of symptoms, etc.

No attempt should be made to self-diagnose or medicate—severe damage can occur from inappropriate treatment. Only the simple "first aid" measures covered below should be instituted by untrained, unlicensed individuals.

An ophthalmologist should be called once it is clear that an emergency situation exists. If not available, a primary care medical doctor may be contacted for advice or referral to an ophthalmologist. Hospital emergency rooms are usually covered twenty-four hours a day by consulting ophthalmologists. Many of the new "walk-in" emergency care centers are also equipped for managing or referring eye emergencies.

Accidents and injuries involving the eyes

Eye injuries are quite common but fortunately do not usually result in significant loss of vision.

Severe ocular trauma with loss of vision or of an eye is quite rare but significantly devastating to warrant special mention and directions for avoidance of such injuries (see Prevention, below).

Management of Eye Injuries

General Measures

First aid for any associated life-threatening injuries should always take precedence over management of eye trauma.

In general, only the simplest, obvious first aid measures should be taken by untrained personnel in the management of eye injuries. These will be discussed below along with the more definitive care rendered by the ophthalmologist.

All of the important details and circumstances surrounding the incident should be noted and any tools, objects or chemicals, etc. involved in the injury should be brought along to the doctor. The time that the injured person last ate should also be noted in case emergency surgical repair under general anesthesia is necessary. Ordinarily 6-8 hours should elapse between eating or drinking and general anesthesia. It is normally good practice to avoid giving food or drink to the injured person in the event that surgical repair may be required.

When other injuries (facial, head, etc.) are sustained at the time of the eye injury, it is best to proceed to the hospital emergency room for thorough evaluation and triage. Obviously, in cases of eye emergencies, someone other than the patient should drive to the doctor's office or emergency room.

Suggested First Aid Kit for Eye Injuries:

- oval eye pads
- bandage tape (non-irritating, hypoallergenic)
- rigid plastic eye shield
- gauze pads
- sterile ocular irrigating fluid (or sterile saline)
- penlight

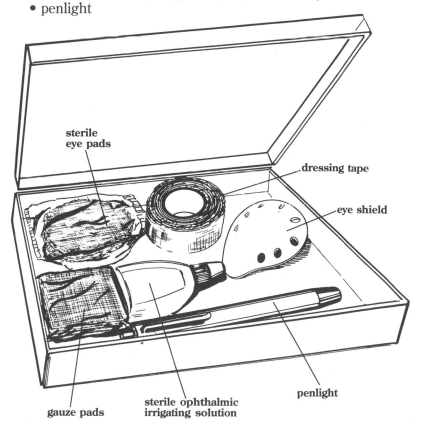

sterile eye pads

dressing tape

eye shield

penlight

gauze pads

sterile ophthalmic irrigating solution

Specific Injuries

Blunt Injuries

(e.g., balls, fist, rocks, snowballs, etc.)

general considerations:
- blunt injuries damage the eye by transmission of the force from the moving object to the ocular tissues. Depending on the size, consistency, mass and speed of the object and its angle of impact, damage may range from trivial to devastating with consequent loss of vision.

- the "blink reflex" is very fast and well developed in most individuals providing a degree of protection for the eye.

- the tissues of the lids are very loose and distensible allowing for considerable swelling after an injury. The swelling often worsens during the first 24-48 hours and may extend across the bridge of the nose to involve the lids of the opposite, non-injured eye.

- blunt injuries to the eyes are often accompanied by nausea, vomiting and lethargy.

first aid and follow-up:
- manipulation of the lids or eyes should be avoided since the eye may have been seriously injured internally or even ruptured.

- no ice or other types of applications should be used without specific instructions from the ophthalmologist.

- ordinarily, eye patches are not necessary and may, in fact, aggravate the injury.

- a pair of sunglasses or protective eye goggles may be used prior to definitive care if they can be fitted without any pressure on the swollen lids. A plastic eye shield, if available, can be carefully applied.

- time and circumstances of the injury should be noted.

- qualified emergency medical personnel or the ophthalmologist should be contacted for evaluation of all but the most trivial injuries.

potential damage:
- *eyelid edema* (swelling) and *ecchymosis* (bruising)

- *orbital "blow-out" fracture.* The fragile bones of the orbit (socket), especially the floor and medial (nasal) wall, can be broken by the transmitted force of the blunt injury. Extraocular muscles and even the eye itself can be trapped in the fracture site. Surgical repair is necessitated in the latter instances. X-rays and/or CT scans are necessary to determine the presence and extent of orbital fractures.

- *conjunctival edema (chemosis) and subconjunctival hemorrhages* are common, usually inconsequential results of blunt ocular injury.

- *corneal abrasions and edema* (scratches and/or swelling of the cornea) can result if the lids fail to adequately protect the globe. Corneal abrasions usually heal without incident after treatment with topical antibiotics and patching. Corneal edema ordinarily spontaneously resolves but can result in some loss of vision if severe and prolonged.

- *iritis (see page 204)* very commonly results from blunt injury and may also cause secondary glaucoma (intraocular pressure elevation)—*see page 164*. Iritis is usually easily managed with "cortisone" and dilating drops.

- *iridodialysis* (dislocation of the iris root from the ciliary body) is a less common and potentially serious result of blunt trauma.

- *traumatic hyphema (see page 172)* occurs if an iris or ciliary body blood vessel is ruptured.

- *paralysis of the pupil* commonly results from significant blunt trauma. The pupil on the injured side may remain permanently more dilated (enlarged) than the opposite side.

- *secondary glaucoma (see page 164)* may result from iritis, hyphema, or direct damage to the drainage angle of the eye, etc. Secondary glaucoma is usually easily managed with pressure-lowering drops and pills. In some severe cases the pressure may be poorly controllable and some loss of vision may occur.

- *traumatic cataract (see page 134)* or **dislocated lens** *(see page 149)* can result from blunt injury and may require surgical treatment.

- *vitreous hemorrhage (see page 206)* usually clears with time but associated ocular injuries may result in some loss of vision.

- *retinal tear (see page 191)*, *retinal detachment (see page 193)*, or *retinal dialysis* (disinsertion of the retina) can occur and ordinarily require surgical treatment.

- *commotio retinae* (Berlin's edema) refers to the extensive patchy swelling of the retina that can occur after severe blunt injury. If prolonged and severe, significant visual loss may occur. Prednisone may be used to help limit swelling and inflammation.

- *macular edema (see page 177)* and macular hole formation can be serious consequences of blunt ocular injury. Loss of central vision can occur from a macular cyst or hole. Medical treatment with steroids and anti-inflammatory agents is not reliable.

- *choroidal rupture* is a break in the pigmented blood vessel layer underlying the retina. If a choroidal rupture involves the macular area, central vision can be lost. Late development of subretinal neovascularization (new blood vessel growth) can occur in areas of choroidal rupture leading to hemorrhage and scarring.

- *optic nerve injuries* (avulsion, transection, infarction, etc.) can occur after blunt ocular injury by various mechanisms including interruption of blood supply, damage from fractured orbital bones, etc. Optic nerve damage is often permanent with significant loss of vision.

- *ruptured globe* (traumatic disruption of the eyeball) is one of the most serious possible results of blunt ocular injury. The sclera (white coat of the eye) is subject to disruption at various weak points. The force necessary to produce a ruptured globe is such that extensive associated injuries usually accompany the rupture and normal vision is often

not salvageable. Emergency microsurgical repair of a ruptured globe and attention to associated intraocular injuries
are necessary if any vision is to be retained.

Sharp Injuries
(knives, hooks, pointed instruments, darts, animal bites, etc.)

general considerations:
- sharp injuries result in lacerations (cuts), abrasions
  (scrapes), and punctures of the various ocular tissues.

- besides the damage done at the time of the injury, further
  complications from infection and scarring can threaten the
  function of the eye and its supporting structures.

first aid and follow-up:
- first aid by untrained personnel for sharp injuries of the
  eye should be limited to the treatment of cuts and
  scrapes of the lids by application of light sterile dressings to stop bleeding and prevent contamination.

- in cases of lid lacerations it is always possible that the eye
  has been injured as well. In those instances where any
  doubt exists about eye involvement no patching or other
  manipulation should be carried out since any existing
  damage may be compounded. A plastic eye shield or other suitable rigid protector may be carefully applied to
  prevent further external pressure on the eye.

- in cases of severe trauma to the eye lids with loss of lid
  substance, every effort should be made to find any ampu-
  tated tissue and to preserve it in ice.

- if possible, the object which caused the injury should be
  retrieved for examination by the ophthalmologist.

- no attempt should be made to remove any protruding
  sharp object from the lids or eyes since this may com-
  pound any existing injuries. This should be done only by
  the ophthalmologist or other qualified medical personnel.

> - as usual, the time and circumstances of the injury should be noted and, depending on the nature of the injury, the ophthalmologist or other appropriate emergency medical personnel should be consulted
>
> - a history of tetanus vaccination should be obtained

potential damage:
- *clean lacerations of the lids* can usually be repaired with excellent cosmetic results and no functional disability. Due to the rich blood supply of the eyelids, infection is not a common problem. Furthermore, the laxity of the lid skin provides versatility for plastic surgical repair techniques. Extensive, jagged and contaminated lacerations are more challenging and may result in cosmetic and/or functional defects and scarring.

- *lid lacerations involving the tear ducts* (located at the corner of the eye near the root of the nose—*see page 8)* can result in scarring and malfunction of the tear drainage system with resultant excess tearing (epiphora). Microsurgical repair of lacerated tear ducts, using special stents or inserts, is often necessary (particularly with lower lid involvement) if normal tear function is to be preserved. Dog bites of the lids result in tear duct damage with alarming frequency.

- *conjunctival lacerations* and conjunctival abrasions are usually inconsequential but may mask associated deeper lacerations of the sclera or extraocular muscles. Only a careful slit lamp examination by an ophthalmologist can determine the full extent of the injury.

- *corneal abrasions (see page 140)*, though usually very painful and associated with temporary reduction of vision, are ordinarily easily managed with topical antibiotics and patching.

- *corneal lacerations* (deep cutting injuries of the cornea) can be much more threatening to vision. If the visual axis (center of vision) is affected, scarring will reduce vision despite microsurgical repair of the laceration. A subsequent corneal transplant may be necessary to restore vision. Even when not involving the visual axis, corneal lacerations can threaten the eye by damage to intraocular tissues, infection, inflammation, astigmatism, etc. Prompt, painstaking microsurgical repair of the cornea and any associated ocular injuries is crucial to achieving satisfactory visual results.

- *isolated scleral lacerations,* not involving other ocular structures can usually be satisfactorily repaired. "Through and through" lacerations involving the underlying choroid and retina require careful attention to all injured tissues (retinal cryopexy and reattachment, etc.) and can, despite all efforts, result in significant loss of vision.

- *lacerations or disinsertions of the extraocular muscles,* unless promptly repaired, can lead to serious disturbances of ocular motility.

- *lacerations or other sharp injuries to the optic nerve* are very rare and visually devastating injuries.

- other possible after-effects of serious penetrating ocular injuries include *traumatic cataract (see page 134),* *endophthalmitis (see page 151),* and *sympathetic ophthalmia (see page 200)* as well as vitreous hemorrhage and retinal detachment as covered above.

Foreign Body Injuries

(metallic fragments, wood chips, air-borne debris, broken glass, etc.)

general considerations:
- foreign body injuries to the eyes are extremely common and usually not very serious if properly treated.

- particles of all types can make their way between and underneath the lids to lodge on the surface of the eye (usually the cornea) or on the underside of the lids.

- many foreign objects, though uncomfortable, are well tolerated by the eye without serious injury for short periods of time. Contaminated or toxic substances can, however, cause serious damage.

- high speed fragments (from hammering, drilling, sawing, weed whipping, etc.) have the potential for penetrating the protective coats of the eye (cornea or sclera) and entering the inner cavities of the eye where serious damage often results regardless of the nature of the material.

---

first aid and follow-up:
- simple attempts can be made by the injured individual to remove casual air-borne debris by alternately holding the lids apart and blinking and rotating the eyes. Frequently, the foreign matter will wash out with the excess tearing produced by the injury.

- no attempt should be made by untrained personnel to remove foreign bodies from the eyes using cotton tipped applicators, fingers or any sort of instruments. More serious injury can result from the attempted removal than from the foreign object.

- symptoms can not be relied upon to determine whether a foreign body is present or not. Often times the object has been extruded from the eye but the "foreign body sensation" persists from a scratch caused by the object. Retained foreign bodies inside the eye may not be felt at all. In situations of suspected foreign body injury where high speed objects are involved, as described above, an examination by an ophthalmologist is imperative.

- persistent "foreign body sensation" must be evaluated by qualified medical personnel. Most emergency room physicians or PAs are capable of examining the eye for the presence of a foreign body and can usually remove superficial retained foreign bodies from the cornea or conjunctiva. If there is any doubt, the individual is usually referred to the ophthalmologist. If readily available, it may be preferable to seek the attention of the ophthalmologist at the outset.

---

potential damage:

- *retained corneal foreign bodies* are, by far, the most common injuries of this sort. Usually the object can be removed by the professional with no adverse consequences. Healing of the tiny abrasion caused by the object usually occurs within a day or so. Corneal foreign bodies lodged in the center of the cornea (in the visual axis) can heal with a small but visually disabling scar. Deeply imbedded corneal foreign bodies can cause defects which heal poorly and lead to recurrent corneal erosions *(see page 190)*.

- another common location for retained foreign bodies is the inner aspect of the eye lids (especially the upper lid). Metal fragments, wood chips and even insect parts are often discovered by the ophthalmologist upon everting the upper lid. Depending on the nature of the object and the length of time it is present, extensive abrasions of the cornea can result from this type of injury. Once the object is removed, however, the abrasions usually heal without incident.

- *retained intraocular (inside the eye) foreign bodies* are far more threatening to vision than superficial foreign bodies. Infection, bleeding, retinal damage, chemical and toxic reactions, etc. can all cause profound and permanent damage to the eye. Complex emergency microsurgical procedures are usually necessary if vision is to be preserved.

Chemical Injuries

(household or industrial acids or alkalis, etc.)

general considerations:

- chemical injuries of the eyes are quite common and, depending on the nature and dosage of the chemical, can be trivial or blinding.

- chemical burns of the eyes and eyelids from acids and alkalis are among the most common and destructive chemical injuries encountered by the ophthalmologist.

- alkali injuries (lime, lye, ammonia, etc.) are usually much more devastating than acid injuries (hydrochloric acid , sulfuric acid, organic acids, etc.).

- other types of chemical eye injuries include solvents (alcohols, ketones, aldehydes, etc.) oxidizing agents (hydrogen peroxide, etc.) and metallic corrosives (salts of silver and copper, etc.).

- chemicals can enter the eye by splashing or spraying, from nearby explosions or by direct contamination from hands or clothing, etc.

- carelessness with household cleaning agents (window cleaners, detergents, drain cleaners, etc.) and automobile products (gasoline, batteries, antifreeze etc.) account for a great many of the chemical eye injuries seen by the ophthalmologist. School and industrial laboratory accidents as well as criminal mischief also contribute to the toll of preventable chemical eye injury.

- prevention is critical to reducing the number of eyes lost to chemical injuries. Awareness of the dangers posed by household chemicals, careful storage and use of these substances and appropriate safety eyewear will all contribute to prevention of the tragic loss of sight due to chemical eye injuries.

first aid and follow-up:
- immediate, copious irrigation of the eyes with tap water or saline solution is critical to the proper management of most chemical eye injuries. No time should be wasted searching for special "eye washes". A sink, shower, drinking fountain or other ready source of water should be used to thoroughly wash  out any chemical residue. Some laboratories and work areas with potential chemical exposure are equipped with special eye-irrigating stations. Familiarity with loca-

tions and use of these facilities is strongly recommended for anyone working with or near dangerous chemicals.

- all but the most trivial chemical eye injuries should be followed up with the ophthalmologist or appropriate emergency medical personnel. Irrigation of the eyes is continued, as necessary, in the emergency room or doctor's office with sterile saline solutions or ocular irrigating fluids to ensure that any residual chemical is removed from the eyes. Bottles or labels describing the offending chemical should be brought along for the examining physician.

- the ophthalmologist ordinarily inspects the eyes and inner recesses of the lids for possible retained particles and assesses the overall damage to the eyes. Besides irrigation, he or she may institute other emergency measures including debridement and even surgery in severe cases. Other emergency medical treatments by the ophthalmologist may include the use of antibiotics, steroids, dilating drops, pressure reducing agents, etc. and special dressings. Hospitalization is usually necessary in severe cases.

potential damage:
- *minor, superficial chemical eye injuries* usually heal quite well with no adverse effects on vision.

- *more severe chemical eye injuries* can result in variable degrees of vision loss from corneal scarring, secondary glaucoma, intraocular inflammation, infection and cataract formation. Eyelid distortion and scarring can also occur.

Thermal Burns

(flames, explosions, hot objects, embers, cigarettes)

general considerations:
- facial burns from flames often involve the eyelids sparing the eyes. Rapid, reflex lid closure and upward movement of the eyes under the lids (Bell's phenomenon) protect the eyes, in many instances, from direct injury.

- hot embers and cigarettes can pass between the lids and cause corneal and conjunctival burns. Cigarette burns to the lids and eyes commonly occur when a toddler walks into a lit cigarette.

---

first aid and follow-up:
- serious, life-threatening injuries always take precedence over the management of eye injuries. Where appropriate, fire and emergency medical personnel are notified and life sustaining first aid is administered. Control of shock and infection are the primary medical concerns.

- in cases of isolated eye-area burns, any residual ash or molten material is carefully wiped away from the lids. Antibiotic (ophthalmic) ointment and a light sterile dressing can be applied for moderately severe burns. No dressing is required for more superficial burns.

- appropriate emergency medical personnel or the ophthalmologist should be consulted for further management.

- in cases of extensive lid burns and loss of tissue temporary protection of the eye can be achieved by the ophthalmologist or emergency medical personnel with cellophane "moist chambers" or the recently available sterile plastic "eye bubbles".

- medical treatment may include antibiotics and steroids where indicated.

- surgical debridement and even emergency skin grafting may be necessary to protect the eyes and reduce the likelihood of infection and scarring.

potential damage:

- *flame burns* most often do damage by destruction and scarring of lid tissue with secondary effects on the eyes. Scarring can occur between the inner aspect of the lids and the eye (symblepharon formation). Damage to the cornea from inturned lashes (trichiasis) and exposure (cicatricial ectropion), etc. can be vision threatening.

- *cigarette or cinder burns* to the cornea, unless very deep or complicated by infection, usually heal without serious consequences.

Radiant Energy Injuries

(sun or sun lamp, arc welding, electric flash, laser, strongly ionizing radiation, etc.)

general considerations:

- ultraviolet light is the most common source of radiant energy eye injuries. UV is, of course, emitted in sunlight and from sun lamps and, in concentrated doses, can cause burns of the conjunctiva and cornea. When ambient sunlight is reflected and enhanced by broad expanses of sea or snow, the threat is multiplied. Oxyacetylene or arc welding light is also rich in UV.

- inadequate protection of the eyes by proper sunglasses, sunlamp goggles or arc welding shields accounts for the many eye injuries of this kind.

- "sun gazing" by psychotic, hallucinating or malingering individuals as well as those watching an eclipse of the sun can produce additional, more serious, injuries to the inner eye (retina and macula) from the longer wavelength infra-red light.

- electric flashes seen in industrial accidents and with electric powered trains and subways can also cause radiant energy injuries to the eyes.

- laser accidents are becoming more common with increasing use of these devices. Improper eye shielding and other safety measures account for most such injuries.

- strongly ionizing radiation (gamma rays, X-rays, etc.) can cause ocular damage over prolonged periods of exposure.

- sunlight, sunlamp and arc welding flash burns of the eyes typically begin hurting several hours after the exposure and many times are not related by the individual to the source. Not uncommonly, the individual with an arc welding burn of the cornea will awaken in pain on the night of the injury unaware of the likely cause of his symptoms. The latent period between injury and symptoms is a function of the intensity and duration of the exposure. Intense exposures have shorter latent periods.

---

first aid and follow-up:
- artificial tear drops provide some temporary mild relief from corneal burns of this type.

- other measures such as anesthetic drops, ointments and patches, etc., should be deferred to the ophthalmologist or other appropriate emergency medical personnel.

---

potential damage:
- *corneal burns (photokeratitis)* are usually very painful but heal within 24-48 hours without serious consequences.

- *radiation cataracts* ("glass blowers' cataracts") can develop from prolonged exposure to infrared radiation (blast furnaces or other sources of extreme heat) but are not commonly seen any more.

- *cataracts* and surface damage to the conjunctiva and tear glands, etc., can also result from other types of radiant energy injury.

- *burns of the retina and macula* from sun or eclipse viewing and some laser injuries can result in permanent loss of central vision.

Prevention Of Eye Injuries

- extraordinary advances in medical and surgical eye care have made successful treatment of many previously hopeless eye injuries possible.

- far more benefit arises, however, from prevention of such injuries.

- following are some specific measures to reduce the incidence of needless vision loss:

  - *keep all potential sources of injury out of children's reach especially strong cleaning agents, chemicals, matches, etc.*

  - *exercise extreme caution when using dangerous chemicals, "jump-starting" cars, operating machinery and power tools, etc.*

  - *wear safety eye wear or goggles when engaged in the use of dangerous tools or chemicals or when playing high risk sports such as racquetball, squash, etc.*

  - *wear appropriate sunglasses or shielding when exposed to intense sunlight, sunlamps, arc welding, etc.*

  - *educate children as to the risks associated with dangerous games using sticks, arrows, snowballs, etc.*

ENCYCLOPEDIA OF OCULAR DISORDERS

AIDS (Acquired Immune Deficiency Syndrome)
   general information—there is currently a tremendous public awareness about AIDS but relatively little has been publicized about the ocular effects of this increasingly prevalent disease.

   AIDS is caused by a virus (the human immunodeficiency virus or HIV) which is transmitted through infected blood or semen. The highest risk populations for contracting AIDS are homosexual and bisexual men, intravenous drug abusers and prostitutes. The virus deranges the immune defense system of the body, leaving the affected individual prey to unusual infections and malignancies. It has been estimated that about three quarters of AIDS patients develop some sort of ocular involvement including retinal bleeding and nerve cell damage, viral infections of the retina (cytomegalovirus, herpes virus) and other fungal and parasitic infections. Secondary involvement of the visual system can also occur from infections of the brain. AIDS virus has been isolated in human tears but there are no documented cases of spread of the disease through infected tear fluid.

   signs and symptoms—vary greatly with the specific form of involvement. Retinal hemorrhages may cause no symptoms but only be discovered on a thorough eye examination. Retinal infections can cause massive nerve cell damage and profound loss of vision. Damage to the visual systems in the brain may cause double vision, limitation of eye movements and partial or severe loss of vision.

   A rare form of cancer seen in AIDS patients, Kaposi's sarcoma, may occur on the lids and be noted as a bluish nodule or on the surface of the eye as a reddish lesion.

   treatment—various treatments are being developed for AIDS but there is, as yet, no cure. There are also antiviral medications used to treat retinal infections with varying degrees of success.

ENCYCLOPEDIA

AMAUROSIS FUGAX

general information—literally means fleeting loss of vision and is caused by episodes of insufficient blood flow through one of the neck arteries (carotid arteries) or its branches to the eye due to clots, emboli (tiny mobile fragments) or spasm. This most commonly occurs in patients over fifty and indicates a significant risk factor for stroke due to the underlying atherosclerosis.

signs and symptoms—sudden, painless, one-sided loss of vision lasting seconds to minutes and occurring either occasionally or up to several times a day. Visual symptoms may be accompanied by more extensive neurologic manifestations including temporary paralysis or loss of sensation on one side of the body and loss of speech (aphasia). The underlying blood vessel abnormality can be defined with the aid of various noninvasive studies and arteriography.

treatment—depends on the exact nature and extent of the underlying problem. Diet, blood thinners, blood vessel dilating medications and carotid artery surgery may all play a role in the management of this disorder.

AMBLYOPIA ("Lazy Eye")

general information—is the term applied to reduced vision resulting from disuse of the eye. It is important to note that amblyopia is **not** a turned or wandering eye **but may result from** an eye turning or wandering.

If a child's eye becomes misaligned (crossed in or turned out, etc.) the brain selectively ignores the image coming from the turned eye and, in time, the nervous pathways from the eye to the brain become underdeveloped and amblyopia results.

A droopy lid covering the eye may also lead to maldevelopment of the visual pathways and cause amblyopia. Other causes include: very unequal refractive errors (e.g., one eye very nearsighted or astigmatic and the other eye normal or farsighted), juvenile cataracts, corneal scars, etc.

Amblyopia does not normally develop once the visual system has matured (after age eight or nine) nor can it effectively be treated once this age had been reached.

signs and symptoms—the presence of one of the conditions mentioned above (wandering eye, droopy lid, etc.) should signal the possibility of coexisting amblyopia. Only a thorough professional eye examination can verify the diagnosis.

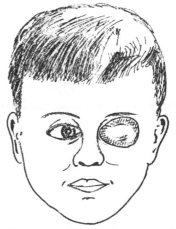

treatment—consists of patching of the "good" or normal eye which requires the amblyopic eye to be used and thus strengthened. The extent and duration of patching depends on the age of the child, the severity of the amblyopia and the response to treatment. Dilating the pupil of the normal eye which blurs the vision in this eye is another means of treatment used in occasional cases where patching is inappropriate or impossible.

Definitive treatment requires correction of the underlying abnormality that originally caused the amblyopia, e.g., eye muscle surgery, prescription of glasses, lid surgery, etc. *(see also page 106)*.

ANISOCORIA

general information—is the term describing inequality of pupil size. A small discrepancy in pupil size (about one millimeter difference) is often normal but this can only be determined by the ophthalmologist. There are many abnormal and some serious causes of unequal pupils.

One of the most common causes of anisocoria is the use of dilating drops *(see mydriatics and mydriatic/cycloplegics—page 84)* in one eye only. This may be for diagnostic or treatment purposes or may be seen in some cases of malingering or hysteria. Occasionally, contact with plants of the belladonna family (jimson weed, nightshade, etc.) can result in contamination of the eye which can cause dilation of the pupil.

Conversely, the use of miotic drops *(see page 83)* which constrict the pupil in one eye only can cause anisocoria with the affected pupil being smaller.

Horner's Syndrome consists of unequal pupils (abnormal side smaller) and a drooping of the upper eyelid on the affected side. This results from a malfunction of the sympathetic nervous system's pupil dilator and lid elevation fibers and may be essentially insignificant or due to a more serious underlying cause.

Adie's pupil (tonic pupil) is a usually benign condition resulting in unequal pupils. The abnormal eye will be noted to have a larger pupil in normal room light.

Third cranial nerve palsies *(see page 201)* can also cause a dilated pupil on one side along with the characteristic lid and extraocular muscle abnormalities.

Injuries of the eyes *(both blunt and sharp trauma—see pages 110 and 113)* as well as certain ocular inflammations (iritis) can also result in anisocoria.

signs and symptoms—in some cases, anisocoria is quite obvious. Many times, however, the discrepancy in pupil size is subtle and only detected in the course of a thorough ophthalmologic exam. Additional findings, such as a droopy lid, may provide the clue to an associated anisocoria.

treatment—is entirely dependent on the underlying cause. Most times anisocoria requires no treatment but only the ophthalmologist, neurologist or other qualified medical doctor can make this determination, sometimes only after further specialized testing.

ASTIGMATISM *(see also page 57)*

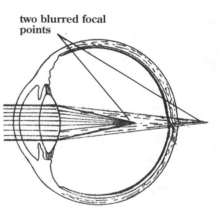

two blurred focal points

general information—is one of the refractive errors of the eye caused by an irregularity in the shape of the cornea (and/or lens) rendering it elliptical or "football-shaped" rather than round. This distorts the light entering the eye and creates a blurred image on the retina. Astigmatism is quite common and frequently occurs along with near and farsightedness.

signs and symptoms—blurred, distorted vision at near, distance (or both) depending on the type and amount of astigmatism. Symptoms of "eyestrain" may also occur. Astigmatism is usually present in both eyes but may be unilateral or asymmetrical.

treatment—if the astigmatism is great enough to significantly interfere with vision or cause ocular discomfort, glasses may be prescribed. The extent of wear depends on the amount and type of astigmatism. Rigid (hard or "gas permeable") contact lenses can correct moderate degrees of astigmatism—standard soft lenses do not. Specialized "toric" soft lenses are successful in many cases.

Various surgical procedures have also been devised for the correction of astigmatism.

BELL'S PALSY

general information—Bell's palsy is a paralysis of the muscles on one side of the face usually thought to be due to inflammation or ischemia (lack of blood supply) of the facial (seventh cranial) nerve within its bony canal in the skull. The absence of associated cranial nerve paralyses helps to distinguish Bell's palsy from other causes of facial nerve paralysis (e.g., tumor, stroke, etc.). A thorough neurologic examination and special testing are usually necessary to rule out associated abnormalities and other specific causes of facial nerve paralysis.

The facial nerve operates the muscles on one side of the face including the muscles which close the eyelid. Paralysis of these nerve fibers results in inability to close the lid and exposure of the eyeball (lagophthalmos).

Bell's palsy can occur at any age but is more common in adults and in diabetics.

signs and symptoms—sudden onset of facial muscle weakness on one side (often on awakening in the morning). There is often associated pain in or around the ear on the same side preceding and for a few days after the onset of the facial weakness.

Drooping of the facial muscles and inability to close the eyelid on the affected side are the hallmarks of facial nerve palsy. Specifically, the muscles of the cheek and forehead cannot contract resulting in asymmetric facial expressions and the upper lip droops, covering the teeth on one side on attempted smiling.

The lids on the affected side may passively close somewhat but part of the eye is usually still exposed and the lids can be easily separated even on attempted forcible lid closure. Tearing is often present due to the absent tear pumping and drainage functions of the paralyzed lid. Blurred vision and symptoms of irritation may develop if the cornea begins to dry out.

treatment—the main concern in managing cases of Bell's palsy is protection of the eyeball from the damaging effects of exposure. The eyelids normally provide a wetting and protective function for the eye and, when paralyzed, allow for drying, irritation, infection and ulceration of the eye. Mild cases merely require the use of artificial tears during the day and lubricating ointments at night. Antibiotic drops and ointments are sometimes also used.

Other simple measures include taping the lids shut at bedtime to prevent exposure and the use of wrap-around protective glasses outdoors to minimize the drying effects of the elements.

More severe cases may require temporary lid suturing (partial or complete "tarsorraphy"). Specialized bandage soft contact lenses have also been used.

Fortunately, most cases spontaneously improve in a few days to weeks. Some severe cases last for many months and never completely recover. Contractures of the paralyzed facial muscles may occur. Various devices have been developed to aid lid closure in unresponsive cases and neurosurgical operations to restore nerve function have been performed with variable degrees of success.

BLEPHARITIS

general information—is the general term for inflammation of the eyelids. This may occur from irritations and allergies, insect bites, infections, seborrhea, etc. Blepharitis may vary from a chronic, mild condition to a severe form with ulceration of the lids and damage to the eyes.

signs and symptoms—depend on the specific type and severity of the blepharitis and may include: itching, swelling, redness, scaling and crusting of the lashes and lid margins. Meibomian gland inflammation and chalazion cysts may develop in association with the blepharitis. Blepharitis may also be part of more widespread skin conditions including seborrhea, acne rosacea, etc.

treatment—depends on the specific type and severity of blepharitis. Mild, nonspecific or seborrheic varieties may simply require warm soaks and daily lid hygiene. Dilute baby shampoo or one of the newer commercially available products can be used for lid cleansing. Other infectious varieties of blepharitis may require antibiotics and/or cortisone creams or even oral antibiotics all of which should only be used under medical supervision.

BLEPHAROCHALASIS

general information—refers to the rare occurrence in the young of excessive, drooping lid skin often as a result of repeated episodes of lid swelling—may also occur as an inherited trait.

signs and symptoms—baggy or droopy lids which may overhang the eye and restrict peripheral vision. Protrusion of orbital fat through the thinned lid tissues may cause localized areas of bulging.

treatment—when restriction of vision or significant cosmetic defects exist, surgery (blepharoplasty) is indicated to correct the abnormality. Both excess lid skin and protruding fatty tissue can be excised.

blepharochalasis

BLEPHAROSPASM

general information—is an involuntary twitching of the lid muscles usually on one side. Stress, fatigue and various metabolic factors may play a role. Periods of lid twitching may last from weeks to months and then spontaneously disappear.

Some severe cases of blepharospasm may occur as part of a hemifacial tic (marked spastic twitching of the muscles on one side of the face). Most often, however, blepharospasm is a benign, self-limited and usually insignificant condition.

signs and symptoms—quivering or twitching of the lid (or lids) on one side due to small muscle contractions. The twitching is often more noticeable to the subject than to an observer.

treatment—most cases of so-called "benign essential blepharospasm" are self-limited and require no treatment. Avoidance of caffeine, cigarettes and other stimulants is advised. Severe persistent cases have been treated by nerve root section and botulinum toxin injection.

BLOCKED TEAR DUCT (Nasolacrimal Duct Obstruction)

general information—one of the most common causes of excessive tearing in infants is blockage of the tear drainage system *(see page 8)*. During gestation in the womb the tear ducts are usually closed, i.e., a thin membrane separates the tear duct from the nasal passages.

Normally, this membrane dissolves by the time of birth and the tear drainage system (from eye to nasal passages) is established. In a small proportion of infants the membrane fails to open on one or both sides and tear drainage accumulates in the tear sac and overflows the lids. Infection often develops due to stagnation of the fluids in the tear sac.

Blockage of the tear duct can also occur in adults but is due to chronic nasal or sinus conditions, injuries, tear sac infections, etc.

signs and symptoms—infants with congenital nasolacrimal duct obstruction usually tear excessively from one or both eyes and accumulate mucus or pus secretions at the inner corner of the eye. The lids may also become somewhat swollen and irritated. There are other important causes of these signs and symptoms such as serious infections of the eye and congenital glaucoma, etc. A thorough ophthalmologic examination is required for proper diagnosis.

Adults with blocked tear ducts also demonstrate tearing and intermittent discharge. Periodically, a severe dacryocystitis may develop *(see page 143)*. There arc, of course many other possible causes of tearing *(see page 152)* and discharge and, once again, a thorough eye examination is necessary for proper diagnosis.

treatment—congenital nasolacrimal duct obstructions are usually treated conservatively with massage of the tear sac, lid hygiene, warm compresses and, if infection is present, topical antibiotics. Most cases improve in a few weeks to months.

If the blockage persists beyond six months of age a "probing and irrigation" of the nasolacrimal duct *(see page 104)* can be performed under anesthesia. There is some controversy as to the best timing for this procedure and as to whether it need be performed at all. Most ophthalmologists, however, still advise probing and irrigation if symptoms persist despite treatment beyond six or nine months. Occasionally, a single probing is not successful in restoring tear drainage and a repeat or more involved procedure may have to be performed.

Blocked tear ducts in adults are more difficult to treat. Occasionally, the passage of special tubes into the tear drainage system is successful. When tearing is unmanageable and/or chronic infection exists a DCR (dacryocystorhinostomy) operation may be performed *(see page 104)*.

CATARACT *(see also page 92)*

general information—the human lens is a disc shaped crystal clear structure situated behind the iris which serves to focus light onto the retina. When the lens loses some of its clarity it is referred to as a cataract. This loss of clarity or haziness frequently develops with age, though the degree of haziness is quite variable form person to person. Many people have some degree of cataract formation by the sixties or seventies and some people develop "age-related" cataracts in the forties! It is important to note that, although most people develop cataracts as they get older, only a relatively small percentage actually require surgery.

There are many other reasons for cataracts to develop (certain ocular injuries and inflammations, various drugs and medicines including "cortisone", metabolic diseases such as diabetes, congenital anomalies, etc.) but the age-related cataract is by far the most common.

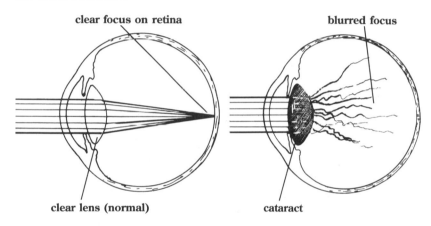

clear focus on retina   blurred focus

clear lens (normal)   cataract

There are many specific types of cataracts named for the location of the opacity within the lens. *Nuclear cataracts* involve the center (or nucleus) of the lens; *cortical cataracts* involve the cortex or substance surrounding the nucleus; *subcapsular cataracts* involve the region just beneath the capsule or "skin" of the lens. *Mature cataracts* involve all of the lens substance.

Various combinations of cataract types often coexist in the same eye. There are many other very specific designations and classifications of cataracts which are beyond the scope of this book. Age-related cataracts usually occur to some degree in both eyes but may be very asymmetrical.

signs and symptoms—visual difficulties are directly related to the location and degree of the haziness within the lens. Very localized areas of cloudiness off to the edge of the lens (e.g., early cortical cataract) obviously do not significantly affect vision whereas a dense haziness of the entire lens (mature cataract) causes profound loss of vision.

Typically, *nuclear cataracts*, develop slowly over many years and may do little more than cause the eye to become more near-sighted ("second sight") which occasionally eliminates the need for reading glasses. Eventually, however, nuclear cataracts can lead to pronounced loss of vision and require treatment.

Cortical cataracts, often progress slowly as well, and affect vision to the degree that the cloudiness encroaches into the center of the lens. Significant glare disability (especially difficulty with night driving) can lead to the eventual need for surgery.

Subcapsular cataracts (especially posterior subcapsular cataracts) are the most visually devastating and often cause great difficulty with reading and substantial glare disability. They also tend to progress quite rapidly (over months) and often require surgery sooner after diagnosis than the other types of cataracts. Posterior subcapsular cataracts are also the type that most commonly occur from steroid ("cortisone") use and in diabetics.

There is a tremendous variation from person to person with regard to resultant visual problems from cataracts. Two people with the same type and degree of cataract may experience very different degrees of difficulty depending on their occupations, routine activities and general attitudes toward vision. Furthermore, the presence and degree of cataract formation in the fellow eye is a significant determinant of visual difficulty.

The severity and natural course of *traumatic* and other *secondary cataracts* depends entirely on the specifics of the case and no generalizations can be made. *Congenital cataracts* (usually occurring from maternal German measles during pregnancy or from rare genetic defects or certain drug ingestions, etc.) require careful examination of the newborn for proper detection. A white or yellowish appearance to the pupil is a clue to possible congenital cataract. Early diagnosis and prompt treatment of congenital cataracts is critical to the development of vision in the affected child.

treatment—In the early stages of cataract development, treatment simply consists of adjustment of eyeglass prescriptions, use of sunglasses and avoidance of situations causing excessive visual disability. Investigation for possible underlying causes is carried out in unusual cases.

As the cataract becomes more advanced, careful consideration is given to surgical correction and a joint decision is made by the surgeon and the informed patient (and family). Cataract surgery in an adult need never be *rushed* unless an unusual complication is present (hypermaturity, secondary glaucoma, etc.). Congenital cataracts, however, do require very early intervention.

Most cataract surgery in the United States is now performed in an out-patient setting under local anesthesia. A variety of surgical procedures can be used and depend on the surgeon's preference and the nature of the cataract. In most instances the cloudy human lens is removed leaving most of the capsule (skin) of the lens in place within the eye (extracapsular cataract surgery). A small exquisitely crafted artificial lens (intraocular lens implant or "IOL") is inserted in the space previously occupied by the cataractous human lens. The IOL replaces the lost "focus power" resulting from removal of the human lens.

Reading glasses (and often thin distance glasses or bifocals) are usually still necessary after the operation. This depends to a large degree on the status of the fellow eye and the visual needs of the patient. IOLs have largely eliminated the need for the thick cataract eye glasses and contact lenses previously required after surgery. (Occasionally, for technical reasons, an IOL is not used and a contact lens or cataract eyeglass correction is substituted.)

Cataract surgery has evolved into one of the most successful operations ever performed. Providing that there is no significant coexisting eye disease there is usually better than a ninety-five percent chance of vision being restored to precataract levels. Complications do, of course, occur in some cases (retinal tears and detachments, macular edema, secondary glaucoma, corneal edema, chronic inflammation, bleeding , infection, dislocation of the IOL, etc.) but most can be successfully treated *(see page 92 for more details and illustrations.).*

A quite common occurrence after cataract surgery, so common (a third or so of cases) that it should not be considered as a complication, is the development of an "opacified posterior capsule" or "secondary membrane". Anywhere from months to years following successful cataract surgery, the posterior capsule or "skin" of the human lens which was left in the eye at the time of surgery can develop a haziness causing symptoms resembling the original cataract. This can very easily be remedied with the YAG laser in a short and painless out-patient procedure. (see page 98).

The term *aphakia* (meaning "without the crystalline lens") refers to the condition of the eye following removal of the cataract. *Pseudophakia* indicates the presence of an IOL implant.

CENTRAL SEROUS RETINOPATHY
(Central Serous Choroidopathy,
Central Serous Chorioretinopathy)

general information—is a "fluid cyst" under the retina in the sensitive macular area which occurs spontaneously, usually in tense, hard driven males aged 35-55. Females can be affected but much less commonly.

Besides the emotional predisposition there is no known specific cause for CSR.

signs and symptoms—rather abrupt onset of blurred, distorted vision in one eye. Images in the affected eye may seem smaller than normal. Both eyes may become affected but not normally at the same time.

Diagnosis can only be made by a careful ophthalmologic exam and may require fluorescein angiography *(see page 39)* for clarification. Most cases are self-limited within two or three months and vision returns to normal. Multiple recurrences sometime develop and complications can occur, reducing vision permanently.

treatment——as mentioned above, spontaneous improvement usually occurs but laser treatment may become necessary in prolonged cases or when rapid restoration of normal vision is critical.

CHALAZION (Chalazion Cyst)

general information—is an inflammation and swelling in one or more of the meibomian glands (oil glands of the lid margin). The openings of the meibomian glands may be seen as tiny pores behind the eyelash roots.

If a gland orifice is blocked, the oil secretions "back up" and a sterile inflammation may develop. Blockages of the meibomian glands may occur in association with acne, seborrhea, allergies, poor hygiene, improper use of eye make-up, and the "meibomian gland dysfunction syndrome" (excess secretion of lipids). An acute infection of a meibomian gland (usually with staph bacteria) is called an acute chalazion or internal hordeolum. This type of chalazion is often loosely referred to as a "sty".

chalazion

signs and symptoms—The chronic, sterile (non-infected) form of chalazion presents as a localized, rounded lump protruding on the skin surface of the lid and is usually nontender. It may be located on the upper or lower lids centrally or in the corners and has a firm, rubbery consistency. Multiple chalazions are not uncommon.

Occasionally a foreign body sensation may be present if there is significant pressure on the eye. Distortion of vision may also occur due to pressure on the cornea (induced astigmatism). Chalazions are more often simply a cosmetic concern. Acute (infected) chalazions are swollen tender masses which occasionally are associated with marked tense swelling of the lid.

treatment—Acute chalazions often respond well to hot compresses and the instillation of antibiotic drops or ointment. Antibiotic/cortisone combinations are also used. Good lid hygiene is also important especially in cases of seborrhea or meibomian gland dysfunction and can be accomplished with dilute baby shampoo lid scrubs or one of the newer commercial preparations (eg., I-Scrub™ [Spectra Pharmaceutical Services]). Unresponsive chalazions may require excision (incision and drainage), a simple office procedure (adults and cooperative children) with local anesthesia *(see page 100)*.

COLOBOMA

general information—a coloboma is a rare condition resulting from a localized failure of development of a part of the eye. During early fetal development there is normally a cleft in the lower part of the eyeball called the fetal fissure. An inherited trait results in failure of any part or all of the fetal fissure to close normally during continued fetal growth and development.

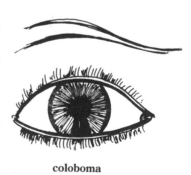

coloboma

signs and symptoms—may be very subtle and insignificant with just a small notch in the iris noted at the lower edge of the pupil. In more severe cases with extensive colobomas involving parts of the retina or optic nerve, vision may be drastically affected. Colobomas usually involve both eyes but are often asymmetrical.

treatment—there is no treatment for colobomas.

COLOR BLINDNESS *(see page 46)*

CONJUNCTIVITIS

general information—is an inflammation of the conjunctiva (thin transparent skin covering the white of the eye and the inside of the eyelids). The specific causes of conjunctivitis are numerous and include infections (bacterial, viral and others), allergies, chemical irritations, skin disorders, contact lens wear, etc.

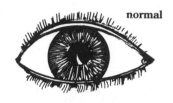

normal

The common designation "pink eye" refers to specific forms of contagious viral conjunctivitis. It is important to

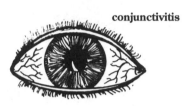

conjunctivitis

note that all cases of conjunctivitis are not "pink eye" and there is no need for concern about the contagion of noninfectious forms of conjunctivitis such as allergic, chemical or environmental varieties.

signs and symptoms—vary with the specific type of conjunctivitis but usually include redness of one or both eyes, discharge (bacterial cases = thick yellow or green ; viral cases = watery or mucoid; allergic = thin watery or mucoid) and variable degrees of itching (especially in allergic cases), burning and blurred vision (especially when the cornea is also involved—keratoconjunctivitis). The eyelids may also be involved in the inflammation (blepharoconjunctivitis) and may be quite swollen. Two varieties of viral conjunctivitis commonly referred to as "pink eye" are:

- *pharyngoconjunctival fever (PCF)*
  commonly seen in children; incubation period of 2-10 days; causes pharyngitis (sore throat), swollen glands, conjunctivitis and fever, usually starts in one eye and lasts up to 3 weeks; second eye may become involved 2-5 days after the first; summertime epidemics may occur affecting children 4-9 years old.

- *epidemic keratoconjunctivitis (EKC)*
  sudden onset of redness, watery or mucoid discharge, foreign body sensation and sometimes pain about the eye, small blood spots may also develop on the eye and swollen,

tender lymph nodes may develop in front of the ear on the same side; incubation period of 8-9 days; usually starts in one eye and lasts from days to weeks depending on the severity of the infection; may be contagious for two weeks and occur in widespread epidemics; second eye may become involved several days after the first; involvement of the cornea causes additional discomfort and blurred vision; some cases develop a form of scar tissue on the cornea which may take many months to resolve.

"giant papillary conjunctivitis" (GPC) is another type of conjunctivitis commonly seen in contact lens wearers, especially with soft lens use. The conjunctiva on the underside of the eyelid becomes inflamed with multiple large "cobblestone-like" excrescences (giant papillae). These can be quite irritating and cause considerable itching, burning and intolerance to the lenses.

treatment—depends entirely on the specific type of conjunctivitis. Bacterial forms require antibiotic drops or ointment; allergic conjunctivitis is treated by removing the offending agent and use of cortisone containing drops or ointment or cromolyn drops; viral conjunctivitis is usually treated by supportive measures (warm soaks, decongestant drops, etc.) but may require steroid and/or antibiotic medication depending on the exact nature of the infection and any complications.

Giant papillary conjunctivitis usually requires limitation or elimination of contact lens wear for a period of time and treatment with cromolyn sodium and/or cortisone containing drops.

Conjunctivitis should never be "self-treated" since use of the improper medications can lead to serious ocular damage in some cases. Always consult your ophthalmologist.

CONVERGENCE INSUFFICIENCY

general information—reading or other close work normally requires the eyes to turn inward toward each other (convergence) as well as to focus clearly on the subject matter (accommodation, *see page 10*). The pupils also narrow or constrict as a part of this so-called "near reflex". In some individuals, the ability to converge the eyes is inadequate (convergence insufficiency).

signs and symptoms—convergence insufficiency is often noted at a time when close work demands are excessive and the symptoms may include blurred vision, double vision, headache, burning of the eyes, tearing etc.

The ophthalmologist must perform the necessary tests and measurements to make a definite diagnosis.

treatment—depending on the severity of the condition and the age of the individual, treatment may consist of special eye exercises, prism glasses or even eye muscle surgery.

CORNEAL ABRASION
general information—is a scratch injury of the cornea, the very sensitive front (clear) part of the eye. The cornea is covered by a very thin "skin" or sheet of cells which, when rubbed or scratched off, exposes the underlying sensitive corneal nerves *(see page 4)*.

Corneal abrasions commonly occur from injuries by fingernails, mascara brushes, tree branches and twigs, paper edges and contact lenses.

signs and symptoms—pain (often severe), foreign body sensation, redness, tearing and varying degrees of blurred vision may all be seen as a result of a corneal abrasion.

treatment—medical attention should always be sought to make the proper diagnosis and determine the extent of injury. Small abrasions may only require some antibiotic drops for a few days to prevent infection. Larger abrasions require antibiotic ointments, dilating drops (to relax internal eye muscle spasm) and a tight eye patch (promotes rapid healing and reduces pain by preventing blinking).

Anesthetic drops and ointments should only be used by qualified medical personnel since improper use of these medicines may delay healing and cause severe corneal damage. Drops and ointments containing "cortisone" or its derivatives should also not be used as they may delay healing and predispose to serious infections.

Most corneal abrasions heal without complications but some result in reduced vision from scar formation and others may lead to recurrent corneal erosions *(see page 190)*.

CORNEAL DYSTROPHY
general information—"corneal dystrophy" is not a single entity but rather a group of different, rare disorders affecting the clarity and transparency of the cornea. By definition, corneal dystrophies are primary corneal disorders, i.e., not caused by prior corneal inflammation, systemic disease or age, etc. Most corneal dystrophies are inherited as dominant traits (i.e., ordinarily one

half of family members are affected). Corneal dystrophies are usually classified according to the layer of the cornea primarily involved *(see page 4)*.

"Epithelial" dystrophies (such as "map-dot-fingerprint" or "basement membrane" and Meesman's dystrophy) affect the surface or skin of the cornea.

"Stromal" dystrophies (such as granular, lattice and macular dystrophies) affect the stroma or middle layers of the cornea.

"Endothelial" dystrophies (such as Fuchs' and posterior polymorphous dystrophy) affect the inside or back surface of the cornea *(see page 165)*.

signs and symptoms—are very variable depending on the specific type of dystrophy. Most corneal dystrophies become manifest by age twenty or so but Fuchs' endothelial corneal dystrophy (one of the more common dystrophies) may not be apparent until the forties or fifties and be first noticed by the ophthalmologist on a routine exam. It may also cause slightly blurred vision and foreign body sensation (due to corneal swelling) prompting the patient to seek medical help.

Macular corneal dystrophy (recessive inheritance), on the other hand, is usually discovered before age ten and can cause profound loss of vision requiring early corneal transplant surgery.

"Map-dot-fingerprint" dystrophy may cause distortions of vision and lead to corneal abrasions and recurrent corneal erosions. Basically, the proper diagnosis and classification of corneal dystrophies can only be made by the ophthalmologist and may require special testing and consultation to pinpoint the specific type.

treatment—depends entirely on the specific type of dystrophy and its severity in the affected individual. The more serious varieties may require corneal transplant surgery.

One of the more common corneal dystrophies, Fuchs' endothelial dystrophy often only requires concentrated salt drops and ointments in the earlier stages to help dehydrate the swollen cornea. The warm, dry air from a hair dryer can often relieve the early morning corneal edema or swelling that occurs. Reduction of the intraocular pressure by various means also helps to minimize the corneal swelling. As the disease progresses and the cornea becomes progressively more swollen and cloudy, corneal transplant surgery is indicated and often successful in restoring vision.

Some forms of corneal dystrophy and corneal scars can now be treated with the excimer laser (phototherapeutic keratectomy or **PTK**).

When a significant cataract is also present, a combined or "triple procedure" (corneal transplant, cataract extraction and intraocular lens implantation) may be performed. Specular microscopy *(see page 37)* and pachymetry *(see page 34)* are useful in monitoring the status of the cornea and in surgical decision making. When corneal transplant surgery can not be performed and painful corneal edema (bullous keratopathy) exists a bandage soft contact lens can often provide comfort *(see page 87)*.

CORNEAL EDEMA

general information—is a swelling of the cornea (front clear part or "window" of the eye). This can result from many different causes including injury, inflammation, inherited disorders, certain eye operations (especially cataract surgery), and elevated intraocular pressure. Depending on the extent and location of the swelling, corneal edema may range from insignificant to visually devastating.

signs and symptoms—scratchy or foreign body sensation (often worse in the morning) and varying degrees of blurred vision are the usual symptoms. An advanced form of corneal edema, bullous keratopathy, may cause severe ocular pain.

treatment—depending on the type and severity of the edema, may include concentrated (hyperosmotic) drops and ointments to dehydrate the cornea. Specialized "bandage soft contact lenses" afford relief from pain in select cases *(see page 87)*. Corneal transplantation may also be warranted. Treatment is also usually directed at the underlying cause of the corneal edema (inflammation, glaucoma,, etc.)

CORNEAL ULCER *(see Keratitis, page 173)*

DACRYOADENITIS

general information—is a rather rare infection or inflammation of the lacrimal (tear) gland which is located behind the upper eyelid on the temporal (outer) side. There are many possible specific causes including viral infections (e.g., mumps), Sjogren's syndrome *(see page 147)* and sarcoidosis, etc.

signs and symptoms—usually include orbital (socket) pain and tenderness in the outer part of the upper eyelid where a swollen mass may be felt. The eyelid is usually swollen and there may be discharge. Occassionally, there may be limitation of motion of the eye with consequent double vision. Only the ophthalmologist or other qualified medical doctor can make the proper diagnosis by examination. The condition may be short lived, improving spontaneously or may run a chronic course.

treatment—depends on the exact nature and severity of the episode. Sometimes, simple supportive care with warm compresses and aspirin may be all that is necessary. Other cases may require treatment of an underlying systemic disease such as sarcoidosis. In cases where an abscess is developing, incision and drainage may be necessary.

DACRYOCYSTITIS

general information—is an infecuon of the tear sac which is part of the tear drainage system. This can be of acute onset or long term chronic duration.

Bactcria multiply in the tear sac obstructing its normal drainage into the nose and causing reflux (back up) of pus or secretions from the puncta (tear drainage pores located at the nasal or inner corner of thc lids). There may be underlying, predisposing abnormalities in the tear drainage system such as strictures or narrowing, polyps, or stones, etc.

signs and symptoms—patients with the acute variety of dacryocystitis are quite uncomfortable with redness, localized swelling and often extreme tenderness between the bridge of the nose and the corner of the eye. In some cases a fistula (direct drainage site through the skin over the tear sac) may develop.

Patients with the chronic variety of dacryocystitis usually complain of tearing and intermittent discharge and sometimes periods of acute infection with symptoms as described above.

treatment—hot compresses and antibiotics (topical and oral) are used to treat the acute form. Significant chronic dacryocystitis may require an operation (dacryocystorhinostomy or DCR) to re-establish drainage of tears through to the nasal passages *(see page 104)*.

DERMATOCHALASIS

general information—refers to the thin, loose redundant skin of the eyelids which often develops normally with age. Premature development of dermatochalasis in middle age can occur as a familial trait.

signs and symptoms—baggy or droopy eyelids—may affect upper or lower lids or both. Upper lid dermatochalasis may be

143

so severe as to restrict peripheral vision. Protrusion of orbital fat through the thinned lid tissues can cause areas of distinct bulging under the skin.

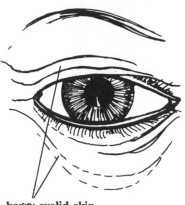

baggy eyelid skin

treatment—When restriction of vision or severe cosmetic defects exist, surgery (blepharoplasty) is indicated to correct the abnormality. Both excess lid skin and protruding fatty tissue can be excised. Care must be taken to exclude medical disorders that can cause or aggravate the condition (thyroid, cardiovascular or kidney disease) and to ensure that no underlying tearing deficiency exists *(see page 103)*.

DIABETIC EYE DISEASE

general information—diabetes mellitus can cause a number of different eye disorders including fluctuations of the refractive error (near- or farsightedness etc.) eye muscle weakness or paralysis and, most importantly, diabetic retinopathy *(see below)*.

Refractive changes are usually in the direction of more nearsightedness (or less farsightedness) when the blood sugar is elevated. This is thought to result from osmotic swelling of the lens with the high sugar levels.

Eye muscle palsies are not common but can occasionally be the first sign of diabetes.

signs and symptoms—relatively sudden and sometimes marked fluctuations in vision can occur, usually in the early stages of the diabetes, when good control of the sugar levels has not been achieved.

Eye muscle palsies can be manifest by sudden onset of double vision and are sometimes accompanied by eye pain. The double vision may be constant or may only occur in certain directions of gaze. Obvious limitation of motion of the affected eye in one or more directions of gaze may or may not be noticeable and may be so subtle as to only be detectable by the ophthalmologist.

treatment—vision fluctuations due to blood sugar elevation are simply treated by stabilization of the blood sugar by diet and medical means.

Eye muscle palsies are usually self-limited, improving spontaneously in weeks to months. Elimination of double vision in the interim can be achieved by covering one eye with a patch or a frosted eye glass lens. Special prism glasses and occasionally eye muscle surgery may be required in persistent cases.

DIABETIC RETINOPATHY

general information—is a disorder of the retinal blood vessels resulting from the diabetic state. The incidence of diabetic retinopathy increases with time, being rare in the early stages and occurring in over seventy-five percent of diabetics after twenty years. Diabetic retinopathy is the leading cause of blindness in the U.S. in adults under age sixty-five.

The blood vessels throughout the body are affected by diabetes, especially those in the eyes, kidneys, brain and extremities. An increase in the permeability of the vessels of the retina leads to leakage of fluid and blood into the delicate nerve structure of the retina (background diabetic retinopathy).

normal retina

diabetic retinopathy

In more advanced stages, new blood vessels begin to develop which are prone to hemorrhage and can lead to scar tissue formation and even retinal detachment (proliferative diabetic retinopathy). When this stage of diabetic retinopathy is reached other serious complications can develop including a severe form of glaucoma (neovascular glaucoma).

signs and symptoms—in the early stages of diabetic retinopathy there may be no symptoms *(see also Diabetic Eye Disease, page 144)*. Only a thorough and careful medical eye examination by an ophthalmologist may detect the tiny blood spots or fatty deposits in the retina (background diabetic retinopathy). Another subtle sign is the presence of microaneurysms which are tiny outpouchings on the retinal blood vessels due to diabetic damage to the vessel structure.

When leakage of fluid or bleeding affect the macula (sensitive central part of the retina responsible for fine vision) loss of visual acuity occurs and may be noted as difficulty with reading or driv-

ENCYCLOPEDIA

ing, etc. A special photographic process *(fluorescein angiography, see page 39)* is very helpful in detecting the subtle effects of diabetic retinopathy. If the condition progresses without treatment, severe visual loss and even complete blindness may ensue. Both eyes are affected although there may be considerable asymmetry between the eyes.

treatment—control of the blood sugar and blood pressure are important but progression of the retinopathy may occur despite all medical efforts. When vision is significantly threatened, laser treatment (argon or krypton laser photocoagulation) can be very effective in slowing or halting the process. Leaky blood vessels can be "cauterized" with the laser (focal treatment) and proliferative disease can be treated by a more extensive application of the laser (panretinal photocoagulation or PRP). PRP involves partial peripheral retinal ablation in an effort to reduce the amount of the chemical secreted by the diabetic retina which causes the proliferative retinopathy *(see page 99)*.

More advanced cases with persistent bleeding into the middle of the eye (vitreous hemorrhage) and scar tissue formation require vitrectomy and other sophisticated surgical procedures *(see page 95)*. Various scientific studies have proven beyond doubt the considerable value of laser and vitrectomy surgery—early detection and proper medical eye care by the ophthalmologist are crucial in the preservation of sight.

DISLOCATED LENS *(see Ectopia Lentis, page 149)*

DOUBLE VISION (Diplopia)
general information—is not a specific disorder but a symptom with many possible underlying causes. Most commonly double vision develops as a result of a sudden misalignment of the eyes such that the two eyes are looking in different directions.

"Monocular diplopia" (i.e., seeing two images from one eye) can occur with cataracts, dislocated lenses, certain corneal disorders, etc.

Children with misaligned eyes (strabismus) easily suppress or ignore the image coming from the deviating eye to avoid diplopia.

Misalignment of the eyes in adults usually occurs from eye muscle paresis (weakness) or paralysis (total inaction) or mechanical limitation of movement (scar tissue, entrapment of muscle in a bone fracture, inflammation, etc.).

Another form of diplopia results from two different image sizes occurring when, for example, one eye is corrected with a thick powerful eyeglass lens causing magnification and the other eye is not (aniseikonia).

signs and symptoms—awareness of two separate images when looking at a single object. Depending on the underlying cause the diplopia may be constant, intermittent or variable. The images may be horizontally, vertically or diagonally separated and be almost superimposed or widely disparate. Diplopia from greatly unequal eyeglass corrections (aniseikonia) results in superimposed images, one larger than the other.

treatment—depends entirely on the underlying specific cause of the diplopia and ranges from watchful waiting to exercises, special prism glasses and, in some cases, eye muscle surgery. When waiting for spontaneous resolution to occur in neurologic cases, patching or covering of one eye eliminates the diplopia.

Monocular diplopia requires attention to the specific underlying cause and may be eliminated, for example, by cataract extraction where cataract was the source of the problem. Diplopia due to aniseikonia (see above) can often be eliminated by the use of contact lenses or other optical measures.

DRY EYE STATE (Dry Eye Syndrome)

general information—tears are constantly being produced by the specialized glands of the eyelids to lubricate and protect the eyes. The amount of tears normally produced gradually decreases with age and many elderly people will experience some symptoms of dry eyes.

A more severe form of dry eye known as *keratoconjunctivitis sicca* can cause significant visual problems. This condition can also occur as part of "Sjogren's Syndrome" which, beside dry eyes, includes dry mouth and one of the connective tissue diseases such as rheumatoid arthritis.

signs and symptoms—burning, foreign body sensation, irritation, dryness etc. are the usual manifestations and may vary considerably from time to time being worse in dry climates and during the winter due to dry indoor heating.

Interestingly, excess tearing may also be an ocassional sign of dry eyes in some people. When the normal tear glands are not producing sufficient tears, reflex tearing may occur from another type of tear gland in an effort to provide adequate lubrication. Contact lens wearers, especially soft lens wearers, may be particularly bothered by even slightly dry eyes and find that their comfortable wearing time becomes very limited.

There are specific signs noted by the ophthalmologist on examination. The tear production can actually be measured and compared to normal values to make a definite diagnosis *(see page 41)*. Other specialized tests can provide additional information regarding the exact type of dry eye state.

treatment—replacement of deficient tears with artificial tear drops is the mainstay of treatment and may be required as often as every fifteen minutes or only occasionally when symptoms warrant depending on the exact type and severity of the dry eye condition. There are many different brands and types of artificial tears. The ophthalmologist can determine the type best suited to a given individual. In addition, lubricating ointments at bedtime are often very helpful. Special mucus-reducing drops and Lacriserts® *(see page 88)* are also sometimes necessary.

More severe cases of dry eyes may require blockage of the tear drainage ducts by tiny plugs or by surgery (laser or cautery). A special type of bandage contact lens *(see page 87)* used in conjunction with artificial tears can also provide relief in certain cases. The use of home humidifiers and avoidance of hot air (e.g., hair dryers, heaters, etc.) are additional simple measures which can be very helpful. Some individuals also find relief with the use of special wrap-around goggles.

The successful treatment of dry eye states can sometimes be a very challenging and frustrating experience and often requires substantial effort and cooperation between doctor and patient.

DYSLEXIA
general information—is a disability involving interpretation of visual symbols. Children with dyslexia have reading problems because of this difficulty comprehending letters, numbers or other symbols. Poor vision certainly can also cause problems with reading, but dyslexia specifically refers to the interpretive disability described above. Many children with dyslexia have perfect eyesight and, conversely, some children with limited vision due to eye disorders may be able to read quite well.

The eyes can be thought of as cameras that "take a picture" for the brain to interpret. The eyes can no more "understand" what is being seen than a camera can understand the picture it is taking. The visual centers in the brain "unscramble" the complex nerve messages sent there from the eyes. A clear picture is of little use without someone to look at and evaluate it. Likewise, clear vision is only part of the whole process involved in reading and understanding.

The exact mechanisms underlying dyslexia are poorly understood. Many children with dyslexia may also have difficulty understanding things that they hear as well as see and dyslexia may be part of more extensive "learning disabilities". Interestingly, many affected individuals have normal or above average IQs. The frustration associated with dyslexia can cause various behavioral disturbances which further complicate the matter.

signs and symptoms—difficulty with reading not caused by a defect in the eyes or eye muscle coordination is the usual presenting feature of dyslexia. Words can be seen clearly but cannot be correctly interpreted and understood. Many children will also have difficulty writing and will often reverse letters or words. More generalized learning disabilities and various secondary behavioral disturbances may also be present.

treatment—a thorough medical eye examination by an ophthalmologist is critical to making a proper diagnosis. Any deficiencies or physical abnormalities in the visual system must, of course, be detected and properly treated. "Mislabeling" a child as dyslexic or learning impaired can do a great disservice and cause delay in the discovery of potentially serious eye disorders.

Parents, physicians and the school system should work together and clearly communicate their observations to one another. Successful "treatment" of dyslexia requires understanding and caring, gentle support. Remedial work by qualified educators and coordinated home assistance are the keystones of proper management. Encouragement of the child in outside activities and athletics is very beneficial in combatting the frustration often associated with dyslexia.

Various other treatments including eye exercises, perceptual training, visual training, hand-eye coordination training, etc. have no scientifically documented basis as proper management strategies for dyslexia unassociated with specific physical abnormalities of the eyes or visual system. These treatments can be very costly and delay the institution of the appropriate remedial programs. Dyslexia can usually be quite successfully managed and resolved by the coordinated efforts of the parents, the ophthalmologist and the school system described above.

ECTOPIA LENTIS (Dislocated Lens, Subluxated Lens)

general information—dislocation of the human crystalline lens can occur from injuries or various disorders of connective tissue (Marfan's Syndrome, homocystinuria, Marchesani's Syndrome, Ehlers-Danlos Syndrome, etc.). The dislocation may be partial or complete.

149

signs and symptoms—double vision or blurred vision can occur from a partially dislocated lens. Extremely blurred vision occurs with complete dislocation. The ophthalmologist makes the diagnosis by slit lamp examination with the pupils dilated.

treatment—depends on the type and severity of the dislocation. In some cases no treatment is necessary. In other cases surgical removal of the dislocated lens may be necessary. Aphakic (post-cataract operation) glasses or contact lenses are sometimes used when the lens has completely dislocated out of the visual axis.

ECTROPION

general information—is an outward turning of the lower eyelid away from the eye. This may occur as a normal consequence of aging in some individuals but can also result from various inflammations as well as chemical and thermal burns (cicatricial ectropion).

The ectropion may involve one or both eyes and can affect the entire lower lid or be limited to a small area of the lid, usually the nasal portion.

signs and symptoms—the diagnosis of ectropion is usually readily apparent—all or part of the lower lid is drawn away from the eye. When the tear drainage punctum at the nasal corner of the lid is turned outward significantly, tears tend to overflow the lid.

The cornea and conjunctiva can become irritated from chronic exposure causing burning and foreign body sensation, etc. *(exposure keratitis—see page 174)*. The inner surface of the eyelid (palpebral conjunctiva) can become rough and reddened from chronic exposure and drying.

treatment—many cases of age-related ectropion can be left untreated providing there are no troublesome symptoms such as excess tearing, burning and irritation, no threat to the health of the cornea and no significant cosmetic deformity.

**ectropion
(lid turned outward)**

When indicated by any of the above mentioned complications, surgery can be performed under local anesthesia as an out-patient, or even in-office, procedure *(see page 102)*.

150

ENDOPHTHALMITIS

general information—endophthalmitis is an inflammation of the internal contents of the eye. In common usage, the term refers to an infection of the inner eye usually subsequent to intraocular surgery or penetrating ocular injuries. Most commonly the infection is due to various types of bacteria but fungal endophthalmitis can also occur.

Rarely, endophthalmitis can develop by blood-borne spread of an infection from another part of the body.

Bacterial endophthalmitis is an extremely serious vision threatening infection which requires prompt recognition and aggressive treatment if the eye is to be salvaged.

Improved awareness and meticulous sterile procedure are making postoperative bacterial endophthalmitis somewhat of a rarity.

signs and symptoms—postoperative bacterial endophthalmitis usually develops within the first three or four days of the operation. Since cataract extraction is the most commonly performed intraocular surgical procedure, endophthalmitis is most commonly seen in the context of recent cataract surgery.

The eye is usually extremely red and painful and the lids are swollen. The diagnosis is usually readily apparent to the ophthalmologist since there are characteristic signs on slit lamp examination.

Rarely, endophthalmitis develops after glaucoma filtering surgery *(see page 93)* at a time remote from the surgery due to infection of the filtering bleb. A seemingly mild infection in such a patient can quickly develop into a serious endophthalmitis. Awareness of this potential is crucial to the proper diagnosis and management.

treatment—central to the proper management of endophthalmitis is appropriate culture and sensitivity testing for identification of the specific strain of bacteria (or fungus) causing the infection. This is normally done in the operating room by aspiration of a tiny sample of the intraocular fluids for laboratory testing.

Potent, broad spectrum antibiotics are usually started simultaneously by several routes: intraocular, periocular, intravenous and topical *(see pages 86 and 87)*. Hospitalization is required for proper diagnosis and management of the infection. Vitrectomy surgery both for culture and treatment may be necessary.

When the culture and sensitivity results are obtained, the antibiotic regimen is adjusted accordingly. Prednisone is also often

ENCYCLOPEDIA

used in conjunction with the antibiotics to reduce the severe inflammatory component of the infection except where fungal infections are suspected.

The results of treatment vary tremendously depending on the virulence of the bacteria and the severity of the infection. In some cases, the eye may be lost; in others useful vision may be salvaged.

ENTROPION

general information—is an inward rotation of the lid (usually lower lid) such that the lashes tend to rub against the eye. Most cases of entropion result from the normal consequences of aging. Other, rarer cases include certain eyelid inflammations, infections or injuries. The entropion may be constant or intermittent.

signs and symptoms—irritation, foreign body sensation, tearing, discharge and blurred vision may all occur depending on the severity and duration of the condition. It is usually apparent by direct inspection that the lower lid edge has turned inward. In intermittent cases the entropion can usually be noticed with forcible lid closure.

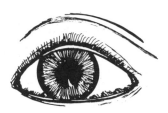

**entropion
(lid and lashes turned
inward)**

treatment—in cases due to infections and inflammations, treatment of the underlying cause usually improves or eliminates the entropion. Some mild cases of entropion can simply be treated by nightly taping of the lower lid to the cheek to pull the lid margin and lashes into the normal position.

More severe cases, especially with significant risk of lash irritation to the eye, require surgery to restore the lid to its proper position *(see page 102)*.

EPIPHORA (Tearing)

general information—excessive tearing can be due to overproduction of tears or poor drainage of the normal tear fluid *(see page 132)*. Overproduction is usually due to irritation, allergy, infection, etc. whereas poor drainage results from either a blockage in the tear drainage system or a failure of the lid or tear drainage punctum to make proper contact with the tear film.

signs and symptoms—excessive tearing can range from mild to constant and profuse. When due to a blocked tear drainage system, the excessive tearing may also be associated with thick secretions and crusting of the lids and lashes especially on arising in the morning.

treatment—is directed at the underlying cause. For example, removal of a misdirected lash, treatment of allergy or infection, etc. will often alleviate tearing due to overproduction. Treatment of tear drainage problems or lid abnormalities is often more complex. Surgery to reapproximate the lid to the eye *(see ectropion, page 102)* or to bypass an obstruction in the tear drainage system is sometimes necessary (s*ee page 104)*.

EPISCLERITIS

general information—is an inflammation of the episclera which is a thin layer of tissue sandwiched between the conjunctiva (skin of the eye) and the sclera (white of the eye). Episcleritis may occur in a "simple" form or a "nodular" form. The condition poses no threat to vision but may be associated with various systemic diseases in up to a third of cases (connective tissue diseases such as rheumatoid arthritis, as well as herpes zoster, gout, etc.). Episcleritis usually occurs in younger people, more often in females.

signs and symptoms—simple episcleritis presents acutely as a red eye. The redness is often localized in patches on the white of the eye as opposed to the diffuse redness seen in conjunctivitis. The condition frequently involves both eyes but may be quite asymmetrical. Mild discomfort is usually present but the eye is not markedly tender as it is in scleritis.

Episodes last one or two weeks and may recur off and on again over a course of three to six years. Nodular episcleritis presents with one or more localized reddish nodules which may be tender to touch and often runs a longer course than the simple variety.

treatment—episcleritis is usually self-limited but resolves more quickly with topical ophthalmic cortisone preparations. Flare-ups may occur on tapering the medication. Nonsteroidal anti-inflammatory agents such as indomethacin are sometimes used in more resistant cases.

ENCYCLOPEDIA

ESOPHORIA

general information—is a tendency for the eyes to turn inwards toward each other. This tendency is usually kept in check by the normal eye muscle coordination mechanisms (fusional control). Many people normally have some degree of esophoria *(or exophoria—see page 158)*. It is only when the degree of esophoria is sufficiently great or the normal fusional control mechanisms of the eyes are inadequate that problems develop.

signs and symptoms—small angle, well-controlled esophorias produce no symptoms and may only be discovered in the course of a thorough eye exam. Larger angle or poorly controlled esophorias may cause intermittent double vision, headaches, "eye strain" and fatigue. Intermittent esotropia (actual crossing of the eyes as opposed to a tendency to cross) may occur and be noticed by friends or relatives. Symptoms from an esophoria are usually worse under conditions of fatigue, stress, overwork, and illness, etc.

treatment—an esophoria that is well controlled, causing little or no symptoms, does not require any form of treatment. Depending on the severity and circumstances of more significant cases (including age, type of work, coexisting eye conditions, etc.) treatment may consist of eye exercises or the prescription of eyeglasses (may be single vision, bifocal or a special type of prism glass). Eye muscle surgery is sometimes indicated for more severe cases unresponsive to all other forms of treatment.

ESOTROPIA

general information—is an inward deviation of the eyes toward each other ("crossed eyes"). Esotropia may be congenital (present at birth) or acquired (develops at some later point in life). Esotropias may be further classified as *accommodative* (related to the focusing of the eyes), *non-accommodative* (also called basic) or *mixed* (combination of accommodative and non-accommodative forms of esotropia).

It is very important to determine which type of esotropia is present since the treatment varies considerably from one type to another. Accommodative esotropia usually develops between the ages of six months to seven years but most commonly occurs between two and three years of age and may simply require the prescription of eyeglasses for its correction. Basic and mixed forms of esotropia, depending on severity and associated circumstances, may in addition require surgical correction. *Congenital esotropia* is usually of the basic variety and often requires early surgical correction to allow for normal development of eye muscle coordination. Improper classification, can obviously lead to serious errors in management.

The causes of esotropia and other forms of strabismus *(see page 199)* are not entirely clear but an important distinction must be made between **paralytic** forms (due to specific nerve and/or muscle weak-

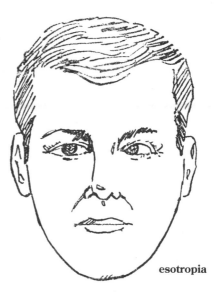

esotropia

nesses) and the **non-paralytic** forms which may be due to a number of different mechanisms which are beyond the scope of this book. Most cases of esotropia (and other forms of strabismus) are of the non-paralytic variety and are actually imbalances *between* the eyes and are not due to a specific faulty or weakened muscle. Both eyes usually tend to turn inward toward each other but in most cases the brain "selects" one of the eyes to see straight and the other to do the turning. Therefore, instead of both eyes turning inward twenty degrees, for example, one eye may actually turn inward forty degrees and the other remain straight.

The same eye may always be the one to turn inward or the eyes may alternate, right eye crossing half the time and left eye the other half. Occasionally, both eyes may actually turn inward simultaneously but this is usually seen in the very large angle congenital turns. In cases where the same eye is always the one to turn, amblyopia is likely to develop *(see page 126)*. **Amblyopia** (also called "lazy eye") is poor vision that results from disuse of the turning eye. Unfortunately, the term "lazy eye" has been incorrectly thought of as being synonymous with turning, wandering or crossed eyes—"lazy eye" is actually a *result* of a constantly turning eye and not the proper designation for the turning of the eye itself.

There is a definite hereditary element to esotropia and other forms of strabismus but no simple generalizations can be made about the chances of a child inheriting the condition. There is, however, a higher incidence of strabismus within families with affected members.

signs and symptoms—crossing of the eyes is common to all forms of esotropia but the age of onset, the amount, frequency and specific pattern of turning are highly variable. Most important is the separation of cases of truly crossing eyes from cases of *pseudostrabismus (see page 187)*. Many infants are born with a broad, flat nasal bridge which gives the illusion of crossing eyes when, in fact, they are straight.

Symptoms of esotropia vary with type and duration of the condition. Intermittent esotropia may cause symptoms of headaches, blurred vision, intermittent double vision, etc. In cases of uncorrected accommodative esotropia, the eyes may appear straight when focusing efforts are relaxed; if an effort is made to focus and clear the vision, however, the eyes may then cross. This type of esotropia, as mentioned above, often develops in a previously normal child at the age of two or three. Congenital esotropia is often a very large angle crossing of the eyes present at birth or within the first several months of life. Esotropia can even develop in an adult as a decompensation of a previously existing esophoria or intermittent esotropia.

treatment—it is very important to note that it is not normal for a child to have crossed eyes. There is a commonly held misconception that children "outgrow" crossed eyes. This probably stems from the fact that pseudostrabismus (see above) does indeed pass with growth and development. A true crossing of the eyes is, however, always cause for concern and for referral to an ophthalmologist.

Once esotropia is diagnosed by the ophthalmologist the specific type must be determined. A careful measurement of the focusing status of the eyes (refraction)is performed using special dilating drops and all other aspects of the eyes are checked to rule out associated physical defects. Careful measurements are also made of the amount and type (alternating, unilateral, intermittent, etc.) of the crossing and the presence or absence of amblyopia is determined. Repeat measurements over time are necessary to fully and properly evaluate a given case of esotropia.

Exact treatment protocols vary greatly depending on the specifics of a given case and the preferences of individual ophthalmologists. The following are generalizations regarding the proper management of esotropias:
- *congenital esotropia* usually requires surgical correction at a very early age (from six months to before two years) to permit the future development of some degree of binocular

cooperation (both eyes working together). The turn should be stable, a number of reliable measurements should be recorded and any associated amblyopia should be first treated by patching *(see page 106)*. Consistent preference for looking (fixating) with the same eye and allowing the other to do the turning indicates the possible presence of amblyopia; free alternation between the eyes for fixation implies correction of the amblyopia. Both eyes are usually operated on and repeat surgery may be necessary in the future.

- *accommodative esotropia* (focus related) is usually managed by prescription of eyeglasses (may be single vision or bifocals depending on the measurements). The turn is not "cured" by glasses since children with accommodative esotropia will still cross without their glasses but will be straight with the glasses in place. Some children may decompensate to a non-accommodative type of turn and need surgery—others do very well and improve spontaneously with time.

- *mixed esotropias* (partially accommodative and partially non-accommodative) require attention to both aspects of the turn and may need to be treated by both surgical and optical (eyeglass) means.

- *basic (non-accommodative) esotropias* of sufficient magnitude (e.g., congenital esotropia) require surgical correction.

- orthoptic eye exercises and special prism glasses also have a place in the management of some esotropias and are used at the discretion of the treating ophthalmologist. Vision training as practiced by non-ophthalmologist eye care practitioners is not discussed here and is not part of the armementarium of the medical eye doctor. Eye exercises of any kind, however, should not be carried out beyond their specific utility and never to the exclusion of surgery or other treatment means when these are indicated.

- special care and modification of treatment protocols is necessary in the management of neurologically impaired children with esotropia and other forms of strabismus.

- management of esotropia and other forms of strabismus is often very difficult due to the age and cooperation level of the affected child. Surgical correction is also not totally predictable from patient to patient and one or more re-operations to correct a turn may be necessary.

- the elimination of amblyopia is critical in the management of all forms of strabismus since even the best surgical results can be lost by the amblyopic eye not having sufficient vision to maintain fixation.

- surgery for strabismus is usually performed under general anesthesia and recovery is often rapid. The eyes are not removed at the time of surgery as is commonly thought. The tiny eye muscles are simply isolated and either shortened (resected) to strengthen them or moved backward on the eye (recessed) to weaken them. The specific selection of procedure and the muscle(s) to be operated on vary with the type and amount of esotropia. Both eyes are often operated on even when one eye has been the originally and predominantly turning eye *(see page 96)*.

- even after successful surgery for esotropia, continued treatment is often necessary to prevent amblyopia and to maximize the surgical result. Deterioration and the need for repeat surgery may occur even years later despite all measures.

EXOPHORIA

general information—is a tendency of the eyes to diverge or turn away from each other. It is usually kept in check by natural muscle tone and reflexes. Fatigue and prolonged use of the eyes can disrupt the normal balance.

signs and symptoms—in adults, when a significant exophoria is present while focusing at reading range or is associated with convergence insufficiency *(see page 139)*, headaches, eyestrain, burning and intermittent double vision may result.

Many people have minor or insignificant exophorias which never cause symptoms and are only discovered on routine eye examination. Children with large angle exophorias or intermittent exotropias *(see page 160)* often do not complain of symptoms and are only detected by a good observer (parent or teacher, etc.) or a careful eye examination.

treatment—depending on the severity of the situation, treatment may range form nothing to exercises, glasses or surgery. Only a qualified ophthalmologist can provide the full spectrum of services that may be appropriate for proper management of exophorias.

EXOPHTHALMOS (Proptosis)

general information—is a bulging or protrusion of one or both eyes. This may result from thyroid eye disease, or from tumors, inflammations or bleeding, etc. within the orbit There are also various congenital abnormalities that can cause exophthalmos.

The orbit *("socket" of the eye—see page 6)* is a limited space bounded by bony plates of the skull. If this space is invaded by any of the substances mentioned above, the eye is pushed outward.

Thyroid eye disease *(see page 202)* is onc of the most common causes of exophthalmos, usually involving both eyes, though it may be very asymmetrical.

Tumors and inflammations (orbital pseudotumor, orbital cellulitis) of the orbit usually cause one-sided exophthalmos. Bleeding and swelling within the orbit from injuries may affect one or both orbits depending on the nature of the injury.

signs and symptoms—severe exophthalmos is readily apparent to most observers. More subtle, early cases are often only discovered by careful ophthalmologic examination.

There are devices to measure exophthalmos *(see page 37)* and special tests *(CT, MRI scans, etc.—see page 41)* to investigate the underlying causes. In some cases, exploratory surgery may be necessary.

treatment—depends entirely on the cause of the exophthalmos. Thyroid exophthalmos may improve with time or, if severe and persistent, may require cortisone treatment, radiation or even surgical decompression. Mild cases only require protection of the cornea with lubricating drops and ointments.

Treatment of orbital tumors depends on the nature of the lesion and may range from no treatment to radiation or surgery.

Orbital inflammations may require antibiotics (bacterial orbital cellulitis from sinusitis or injuries) or cortisone treatment (orbital pseudotumor).

A comprehensive, multispecialty approach may be necessary in some cases for the best management.

EXOTROPIA

general information—is an outward deviation of the eyes away from each other. Exotropia may occur at birth or develop later in childhood. There is actually a spectrum ranging from exophoria *(tendency to turn—see page 158)* through intermittent exotropia to constant exotropia. The degree of the underlying turn and the individual's compensations and adaptations determine whether the turn is kept in check or becomes manifest. Most exotropias result from an imbalance between the eyes and either eye may, in turn, wander outward (alternating exotropia). When one eye is the habitually wandering eye, amblyopia *(see page 126)* may result.

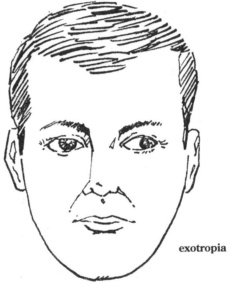

exotropia

signs and symptoms—exophoria, at one end of the spectrum may cause headaches and "eye strain", etc. When the exophoria breaks into an actual turn, double vision may result. Children with intermittent exotropia often develop certain sensory adaptations that allow them to suppress or ignore the image from the wandering eye and will not notice double vision. During periods when the eyes are straight, suppression is absent and the eyes both see normally as a team.

Because of suppression or amblyopia, children and adults with constant exotropia do not usually complain of any symptoms unless the turn is of recent onset from an injury or eye muscle paralysis, etc.

Light sensitivity (photophobia) is a common complaint in cases of exophoria and intermittent exotropia. Bright sunlight is uncomfortable and can disrupt the delicate eye muscle balance.

treatment—the goals of any treatment for exotropia are to relieve symptoms (eye strain, double vision, headaches, etc), improve single binocular vision (use of the eyes as a team) and, where necessary, to improve cosmetic appearance.

In some cases, certain eye exercises and/or glasses may be sufficient. More serious cases with frequent symptoms and large angle turns require surgical correction. The exact timing and choice of procedures are dependent on the specifics of a given case. Infants with constant, large angle turns need surgery at an early age to allow for normal development of the visual system. Older children with infrequent turns and little or no symptoms are usually observed and reexamined at regular intervals. If the exotropia becomes more frequent (e.g., 50% of the time or more) or symptoms are becoming more troublesome, surgery may be necessary. Most surgeons prefer to wait until at least four or five years of age prior to surgery in these instances to allow for further maturation of the visual system. Overcorrections, resulting in esotropia or crossed eyes are more likely to be a problem in very young children with immature visual systems.

Surgery for exotropia in adults must be considered and performed with particular caution since over corrections can result in prolonged, disabling double vision *(diplopia—see page 146)*.

EYELID LESIONS

general information—a number of different growths or lesions can occur on the eyelids as well as other areas of the skin. A summary of the more commonly encountered lesions follows:

- **Basal cell carcinoma**
  is the most common malignant eyelid tumor. The appearance may vary greatly but is usually well localized and slowly growing. These growths are also commonly seen on other sun exposed parts of the body and are more common in the elderly. These skin cancers can eventually spread locally to cause serious damage but they do not ordinarily spread by distant metastases to other organs. The appropriate treatment is excision or removal by any of a number of techniques at the ophthalmologist's discretion. This is usually curative but care must be taken to excise the entire lesion.

- **Chalazion** *(see page 136)*

- **Hordeolum** *(see page 169)*

- **Keratosis**

  may be of the "seborrheic" or "senile" variety. The former appears as an oily, brownish, slightly raised lesion while the latter is seen on sun-exposed areas and may be flat, scaly or raised. This type of keratosis may develop into a more serious skin cancer. Treatment is by simple excision or freezing.

- **Papilloma**

  a benign skin growth caused in many cases by a virus. Size and appearance are quite variable. More serious malignant lesions may also have a papilloma-like appearance. Papillomas may disappear spontaneously or may require simple excision if cosmetically or otherwise disturbing.

- **Sebaceous cyst**

  a benign lesion due to blockage of an oil gland of the skin. Appears as a small round yellowish, slightly raised growth which may spontaneously shrink or require simple incision and drainage.

- **Squamous cell carcinoma**

  a malignant skin cancer that, very occasionally, involves the lids and can spread locally and by metastases. Appearance is quite variable and growth is usually slow. Treatment is surgical excision.

- **Sty** *(see page 169)*

- **Xanthelasma**

  a soft yellowish patch (single or multiple) usually located in the nasal (inner) corner of the lids. May be associated with elevated blood cholesterol levels. This is a benign lesion and need only be removed if cosmetically unacceptable.

FARSIGHTEDNESS *(see Hyperopia, page 170)*

FOURTH (TROCHLEAR) CRANIAL NERVE PALSY
(Superior Oblique Palsy)

  general information—is a paralysis of the nerve which operates the superior oblique muscle of the eye. This muscle has a very restricted field of action mainly working to depress or lower the eye as it moves toward the nose. Fourth nerve palsies may occur at birth or develop later in life and involve one or both eyes. The most common cause is head injury but tumors, diabetes, vascular insufficiency and inflammations may also precipitate a fourth nerve palsy. Fourth nerve palsies may also occur in association with other cranial nerve palsies.

signs and symptoms—double vision is the major symptom in a recent-onset fourth nerve palsy in an adult. The two images are usually vertically or diagonally separated and become even further separated as the affected eye moves toward the nose. Compensatory head tilting postures often develop in children with fourth nerve palsies and may be mistakenly diagnosed as primary neck problems.

treatment—initially, patching of the eye to avoid double vision is instituted. In some cases special prism glasses may eliminate the double vision; others require eye muscle surgery to restore function.

GLAUCOMA

general information—is actually a *group* of disorders which have, in common, excessive pressure within the eye, consequent damage to the optic nerve and loss of some part of the visual field *(see page 40)*. There are many different types and degrees of severity.

ENCYCLOPEDIA

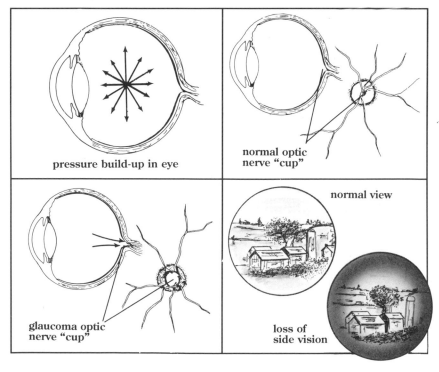

pressure build-up in eye

normal optic nerve "cup"

glaucoma optic nerve "cup"

normal view

loss of side vision

The most common variety is *primary open angle glaucoma* (POAG) also called *chronic open angle* and *chronic simple glaucoma*. This type of glaucoma often occurs after age forty and frequently in the context of a positive family history but may occur in younger individuals with no affected family members. A much less common variety is *chronic narrow angle glaucoma* which can lead to *acute angle closure glaucoma*.

The "angle" referred to in these terms is the angle formed by the cornea and iris *(see page 2)* which contains the fluid drainage meshwork of the eye. In narrow and closed angle glaucoma, the iris partially or completely occludes the drainage angle resulting in pressure build-up—in open angle glaucoma there is a microscopic blockage within the meshwork.

Secondary glaucomas result form some other cause such as inflammation (iritis) or injury, etc. There are also forms of *congenital, infantile* and *juvenile glaucoma* but these are quite rare.

signs and symptoms—in primary open angle glaucoma symptoms are usually absent or very subtle until the disorder has progressed to the point where extensive loss of peripheral vision (side vision) becomes noticeable.

Chronic narrow angle glaucoma may be marked by intermittent periods of eye pain and blurred vision but is also often "silent".

Acute angle closure glaucoma can cause sudden painful loss of vision, headache and nausea and is sometimes mistaken for a gastrointestinal disorder especially when vision loss is minor. The eye, in these cases, is usually quite inflamed. Although both eyes may be predisposed, the acute attack ordinarily occurs in one eye at a time.

Congenital glaucoma is characterized by enlarged eyes, cloudy corneas and excessive tearing in the affected infant.

The various secondary glaucomas present in very variable fashion depending on the underlying cause.

Only the ophthalmologist can make the proper diagnosis. Measurements of the intraocular pressure, charting of the peripheral vision on a computer and analysis of the optic nerve appearance, as well as other special tests are all part of the proper glaucoma evaluation. A "glaucoma screening" consisting of only an "air-puff" tonometer measurement is inadequate.

Many people have borderline results on glaucoma testing and are considered "glaucoma suspects" and carefully followed for signs of progression into true glaucoma.

treatment—primary open angle glaucoma is treated with various types of drops *(see page 83)* and, when necessary, pills. When drops and oral medication are ineffective or poorly tolerated, a safe and effective laser treatment is used *(see page 97)*. In advanced, unresponsive cases with progressive or threatened loss of vision, a "filtering operation" can be performed to help reduce intraocular pressure (s*ee page 93)*.

Narrow angle glaucoma can sometimes be managed by drops but often requires a simple laser procedure (peripheral iridotomy) for definitive treatment. Angle closure glaucoma requires immediate emergency measures to lower pressure followed by the performance of a peripheral iridotomy *(see page 98)*.

Congenital glaucoma also requires very prompt surgical attention if there is to be any hope of saving vision.

The various secondary glaucomas require treatment of the underlying disorder as well as specific medical measures to lower the intraocular pressure.

The use of antihistamine and anticholenergic medications (many cold and allergy medicines, various tranquilizers and motion sickness pills, etc.) should be avoided in cases of narrow angle or angle closure glaucoma prior to iridotomy.

Most cases of glaucoma can be well managed with avoidance of significant visual loss. Early detection, proper treatment and patient compliance with the treatment are the keys to success.

GUTTATA (Cornea Guttata)

general information—guttata are tiny nodules of degenerative material on the back (endothelial) surface of the cornea. Guttata are seen as part of Fuchs' endothelial corneal dystrophy *(see page 140)* but can also develop secondary to corneal inflammation and aging.

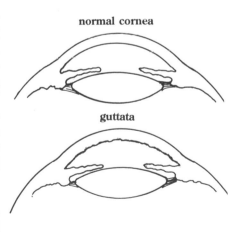

normal cornea

guttata

signs and symptoms—mild guttata unassociated with Fuchs' dystrophy are usually inconsequential and only discovered as part of a thorough eye examination. When very extensive, guttata can lead to corneal edema (swelling) and decompensation. Corneal edema manifests itself as blurred vision (usually worse in the morning upon awakening) and foreign body sensation. Surgical trauma and coexisting glaucoma or intraocular inflammation may aggravate the tendency to corneal edema.

treatment—guttata do not require any treatment unless corneal edema develops. See the section on treatment of Fuchs' corneal dystrophy *(page 141)* for details on management of corneal edema secondary to guttata.

HEMIANOPIA

general information—literally means "half-vision". This may involve one or both eyes and be vertical (altitudinal) or horizontal.

Hemianopias most commonly results from neurologic abnormalities (strokes, tumors, etc.) as well as certain eye disorders such as blood vessel blockages *(see, e.g., ischemic optic neuropathy, page 183)*.

Hemianopias following strokes usually affect one side of the field of vision of both eyes. For example, a stroke involving the visual pathways on the **right** side of the brain may cause a loss of vision on the **left** side of **both** eyes. This can be understood in light of the anatomy of the brain and visual pathways *(see page 6)*.

signs and symptoms—depending on the severity ("depth") of the abnormality, patients with hemianopia may be unaware of their visual deficit and be at significant risk for accidents and injuries. Any individual suffering a stroke should be carefully tested by the ophthalmologist for visual field abnormalities.

Some patients experience difficulty reading, being unable to properly "track" across the page in cases of right sided hemianopia or being unable to find the next lower line of print in cases of left sided hemianopia.

Vertical (altitudinal) hemianopias (affecting one eye only) are usually quite apparent to the individual especially when covering the "good" eye. The top or bottom of viewed objects is often noted as "missing".

treatment—is entirely limited to evaluation and treatment of the underlying causitive condition. In many cases, the hemianopia improves with time as damaged brain and nerve tissue regains function.

Severe brain or nerve tissue damage, however, often leads to a permanent hemianopia requiring modification of daily activities and job responsibilities. Special care must be taken to look to the affected side by turning the head rather than depending on the natural peripheral vision.

HERPES SIMPLEX KERATITIS

general information—herpes simplex is a DNA virus responsible for a number of different infections. There are two main types of herpes simplex virus, one affecting the eyes and lips ("cold sores") and the other causing venereal infection. Eye infection with herpes simplex occurs in many forms and degrees of severity from trivial to devastating and even blinding.

There is normally an initial or primary infection which may go unnoticed and occur in the very young. Most instances of herpes simplex eye infections in adults are secondary or recurrent forms. The virus particles actually lay dormant in the cells of the eye and its sensory nerves and are reactivated to cause infection during times of stress, illness, and excessive sunlight exposure, etc.

signs and symptoms—the initial or primary infection may be manifest by blisters on the skin of the lids, conjunctivitis and keratitis. A recurrence of the infection induced by the factors mentioned above may take the form of corneal ulceration ("dendritic", "geographic" or "ameboid" ulcers) or diffuse corneal inflammation and swelling ("disciform keratitis") as well as other rarer forms of involvement.

Symptoms of recurrent corneal ulcerative disease usually include pain, light sensitivity and tearing. The eye is usually red and the lids somewhat swollen. The correct diagnosis can only be made by an ophthalmologist and may, in fact, be quite questionable at times due to the extreme variation in appearance of some recurrent corneal herpes infections. Special viral cultures are sometimes necessary to make a definitive diagnosis.

treatment—depends on the exact nature and severity of the infection. Some cases respond to simple swabbing of the ulcer (debridement) and/or the use of antiviral drops or ointments. Other cases may require prolonged treatment using various combinations of medications. Severe infections with threatened or actual perforation of the cornea require corneal transplant surgery.

Some individuals experience multiple recurrences over many years while others may suffer only a single episode.

ENCYCLOPEDIA

HERPES ZOSTER OPHTHALMICUS (Shingles)

general information—is a viral infection which spreads along the nerves due to the same virus that causes chicken pox in children (the zoster/varicella virus). Primary exposure in the susceptible child results in the typical picture of chicken pox; reactivation of this virus lying dormant in the nerve roots in an adult results in the picture of "shingles".

The neck, shoulders, and trunk are often affected but when the forehead and lids are involved (first division of the trigeminal nerve) the resulting infection is termed "herpes zoster ophthalmicus". Zoster usually occurs after age fifty but may occur in younger age groups.

A precipitating factor may have been present which upsets the balance of the individual's immunity and allows for the multiplication and spread of the virus. Tumors, leukemia, Hodgkin's Disease, cortisone or chemotherapy treatment, etc. are some of the possible inciting factors leading to the development of shingles. Exposure to the chicken pox virus has also been reported as precipitating a case of shingles.

The main concern in cases of herpes zoster ophthalmicus is the possible involvement of the eye in the infection which can sometimes lead to serious consequences.

signs and symptoms—the actual rash or eruption of zoster is often preceded by a period of malaise, fever, headache and pain or hypersensitivity of the skin in the area of the future eruption. The rash consists of multiple weeping blisters and pustules with red and tender surrounding skin. The skin lesions eventually dry and form crusts. The distribution of the rash is strikingly limited to one side of the body. In the case of herpes zoster ophthalmicus a sharp demarcation between normal and infected skin exists directly down the middle of the forehead.

Eye involvement takes many forms and may range from slight and insignificant to disastrous. A mild conjunctivitis with watery discharge and slightly blurred vision is not uncommon nor particularly serious but involvement of

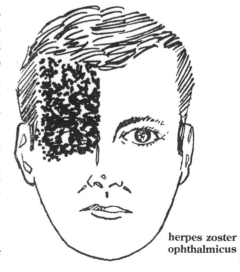

herpes zoster ophthalmicus

168

the cornea (keratitis), episclera and sclera (episcleritis and scleritis) and iris (iritis) may be much more troublesome. The optic nerve and extraocular muscles may also be involved and lead to profound loss of vision. The lids may also be affected to varying degrees. Healing may occur with scarring and malposition of the lids and lashes with consequent irritation of the eye.

Chronic pain and tenderness (post herpetic neuralgia) may develop after healing in some individuals.

Initial evaluation should be made by a team consisting of an ophthalmologist, dermatologist and internist (generalized health factors).

treatment—various ointments (antiviral and antibiotic) have been recommended for the skin. The management of eye problems depends on the specific degree of involvement and may include antibiotic and cortisone containing medication and drops to dilate the pupil. Care must be taken to slowly taper (sometimes over many months) cortisone containing drops to avoid relapses. The treatment of ocular involvement should always be rendered by a qualified ophthalmologist.

Sight-threatening or other serious zoster infections sometimes require oral prednisone or other cortisone containing medicine as well as new antiviral medications.

Postherpetic neuralgia may be very difficult to treat and require prolonged use of medication.

HORDEOLUM (External Hordeolum, Sty)

general information—is an infection in one of the lash follicles or the oil glands leading into one of the lash follicles (glands of Zeiss). This usually occurs from staph bacteria and is commonly referred to as a "sty".

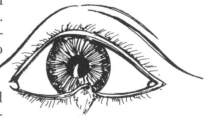

hordeolum (sty)

signs and symptoms—localized area of swelling, redness and tenderness along the lid margin (upper or lower). Marked swelling of the entire lid may also occur.

treatment—hot compresses and topical antibiotics usually provide prompt relief but incision and drainage is sometimes necessary.

HYPEROPIA (Farsightedness)

general information—is one of the refractive errors of the eye due to a relatively flat curvature of the cornea , a smaller than normal length of the eye or both *(see pages 56 and 57)*.

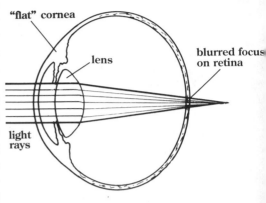

Objects at long distances are seen more clearly than those at close range. The degree of hyperopia can vary widely as can the age of onset and rate of progression. Children can be significantly farsighted but, due to their tremendous focus range *(amplitude of accommodation—see page 10)*, may not experience any difficulty. Unlike nearsightedness, farsightedness can be temporarily "corrected" by a focusing effort of the eye. As the eye ages, however, the focus range (accommodation) decreases and the farsighted person begins to note a blurring of vision at close range and eventually at all ranges—even long distance!

Hyperopia is essentially normal in the newborn and in young children but often tends to lessen as the eye grows in size. In the many others where hyperopia persists throughout life, it may escape detection until later years when accommodation is failing. The anatomic characteristics of the eye which cause the hyperopic state appear to be inherited.

A high degree of hyperopia can predispose an individual to narrow angle glaucoma *(see page 164)* and should be checked for especially throughout later life.

signs and symptoms—blurred vision, more so at close range is the primary symptom *(see also presbyopia, pages 57 and 186)*. Depending on the degree of hyperopia and the age of the individual, intermediate range and distance vision may also be blurred. Tired, irritated or burning eyes, "eyestrain" and headache may alternately or additionally be primary symptoms. Some hyperopic children may exhibit a form of crossed eyes *(see accommodative esotropia, page 154)* resulting from the excessive focusing efforts they exert to clear their vision.

treatment—in children with good vision, normal eye muscle balance and no symptoms, no treatment is necessary. Some hyperopic individuals only require reading or close range glasses. With more substantial degrees of hyperopia and with increasing age, distance glasses may also become necessary. Bifocals provide a convenient means of correcting both the near and distance vision with one pair of glasses. Depending on the circumstances, trifocals and "progressive addition" lenses *(see pages 57 to 59)* may also be prescribed. Surgical correction is less commonly performed for hyperopia as compared to myopia.

HYPERTENSIVE RETINOPATHY

general information—is a disorder of the retina (visual nerve cell layer) resulting from damaged retinal blood vessels secondary to high blood pressure. The severity and duration of the high blood pressure determine whether and to what extent hypertensive retinopathy develops.

Early, mild hypertensive retinopathy may only consist of some narrowing and hardening of the blood vessels. Later on, bleeding and exudation of fluids into the retina may occur. Severe hypertensive retinopathy can be visually devastating and reflects a serious underlying threat to other body systems (heart, brain, kidneys, etc.)

signs and symptoms—many patients with even advanced hypertensive retinopathy have little or no visual symptoms. If bleeding or fluid leakage into the center of the retina (macula) has occurred, vision will be affected. In advanced cases, markedly reduced vision and headaches may occur. Only an ophthalmologist or other experienced medical doctor can make the proper diagnosis.

treatment—is limited to treatment of the underlying hypertension.

HYPERTROPIA

general information—is a vertical misalignment of the eyes where one eye is higher than the other. Hypotropia is the term applied to a vertical misalignment where one eye is lower than the other. Vertical misalignments are less common than horizontal misalignments (esotropia and exotropia) and can occur separately or in association with a horizontal turn. Hypertropias, furthermore, may be part of an inborn muscle coordination problem or result from neurological (strokes, muscle palsies, etc.) or mechanical (injuries, thyroid disease, etc.) causes.

signs and symptoms—sudden onset of hypertropia usually causes disturbing double vision with one image seen above the other. The degree of double vision may vary depending on the direction of gaze. Young children with hypertropia often "suppress" one of the two images and do not report double vision. Depending on the type and degree of hypertropia an obvious misalignment of the eyes may or may not be noticeable to the casual observer.

treatment—significant hypertropias seen as part of a pediatric eye muscle coordination problem not uncommonly require surgical correction. Other cases, especially slight, persistent misalignments in adults may be successfully treated with special prism glasses to eliminate the double vision. In cases where spontaneous resolution of the misalignment is expected, simple patching of one of the eyes temporarily eliminates the double vision.

HYPHEMA

general information—is bleeding within the anterior chamber of the eye. This usually results from an injury to the eye but may also result from abnormally leaky blood vessels on the iris or in the anterior chamber angle (see *page 2*). Hyphemas can also develop during or after some eye operations.

Blood in the anterior chamber may lead to elevation of the intraocular pressure (secondary glaucoma) and blood staining of the cornea. Injuries sufficient to cause a hyphema may also lead to associated intraocular damage such as traumatic cataract, dislocation of the lens, retinal detachment, etc.

signs and symptoms—sudden reduction of vision (may be slight or pronounced) immediately following an injury to the eye and the presence of a visible blood level in the anterior chamber characterize a traumatic hyphema. The blood level may be barely detectable or fill the entire anterior chamber (black ball hyphema).

The ophthalmologist is best suited to make the diagnosis and to examine for associated injuries and complications. Emergency room personnel, doctors in other

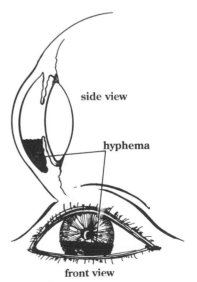

side view

hyphema

front view

specialties and non-medical eye care practitioners should not be relied upon in these circumstances to diagnose and treat since they lack the proper equipment, training and experience.

treatment—restricted activity and close monitoring for complications are critical in the management of hyphemas. Severe injuries with a large amount of bleeding usually require hospitalization. Small hyphemas can often be safely managed in an outpatient setting if both patient and family can be relied upon to restrict activities.

The most dangerous period for a resolving hyphema is from day three to day five during which time a rebleed may occur seriously threatening the eye. Daily examination and pressure checks by the ophthalmologist are necessary to avoid complications. Most small, uncomplicated hyphemas resolve with restoration of normal vision. Larger hyphemas and those associated with other intraocular injuries may carry a guarded prognosis.

Elevated intraocular pressure can usually be managed with medication. If a hyphema fails to reabsorb and poses a serious threat to the eye, surgical intervention to drain the clot is sometimes indicated.

IRITIS *(see Uveitis, page 204)*

KERATITIS
 general information—is an inflammation of the cornea (front clear part of the eye) and is often associated with an inflammation of the conjunctiva *(see conjunctivitis, page 138)*. Following are some of the possible causes of keratitis:
- *infections*
 bacterial, viral, fungal, chlamydial, etc.—can, in some cases, lead to serious corneal ulcers (deep depressions or erosions)

- *chemical irritants*
 e.g., aerosols, certain gases, cleaning agents, preservatives in eye drops, etc.

- *physical irritants*
 exposure to ultraviolet light, arc welding, contact lens overwear, inturned lashes, foreign particles, etc.

- *exposure*
 ectropion, lid paralysis, thyroid eye disease, etc.

- *dry eye states (see page 147)*

- *miscellaneous*
  nerve damage (neurotrophic), SLK (superior limbic kerato-conjunctivitis), allergies (vernal keratoconjunctivitis), Thygeson's superficial keratitis, acne rosacea, etc.

signs and symptoms—burning and foreign body sensation, itching, redness, reflex tearing and blurred vision characterize most cases of keratitis. The severity and duration of symptoms and associated findings vary with the specific cause of the keratitis.

treatment—depends on the specific cause of the keratitis:
- *infections*
  treated with antibiotics or antivirals, etc.

- *chemical irritants*
  treated by removing the offending agent and ophthalmic cortisone preparations

- *physical irritants*
  treated by removal of the offending agent and by combinations of antibiotic and cortisone medications

- *exposure*
  treated by correction of the underlying defects (e.g., lid surgery, etc.)

- *dry eye state*
  treated by proper rehydration of the eyes (*see page 148)*

- *miscellaneous*
  treatment depends on the specific cause

KERATOCONUS
general information—is a thinning and distortion in the shape of the cornea usually first noted in the teens or twenties. The thinning results in the gradual development of a somewhat cone-shaped cornea which can markedly impair vision.

Keratoconus usually involves both eyes but may be very asymmetrical.

Males and females are affected approximately equally, though recent studies point toward a slight male predominance. There have been reports of inherited cases of keratoconus but the actual cause is still unknown.

signs and symptoms—blurred vision is the primary symptom. The ophthalmologist makes the specific diagnosis by special measurements *(retinoscopy, keratometry, keratoscopy, etc.—see pages 32 to 34)*.

Keratoconus can develop gradually and progress slowly and then stabilize in many individuals. Others undergo a rapid progression with drastic reduction of vision. The thinning can sometimes lead to episodes of *acute corneal hydrops* where the cornea suddenly swells with a profound drop in vision. These episodes can be self-limited or can lead to chronic corneal edema and scarring.

treatment—in the early stages, eyeglasses can correct for the corneal astigmatism resulting from the keratoconus. More advanced cases require contact lens correction, sometimes with a specially developed series of lenses made specifically for keratoconus. The contacts do not help correct the underlying condition but only serve to focus the vision to the best possible degree.

In some cases, where the visual improvement from contacts is not adequate or is unsuccessful for reasons of comfort or compliance, surgery may be necessary. Corneal transplantation is very effective in cases of keratoconus but contact lenses are still often required postoperatively for the correction of residual astigmatism. There are other special surgical procedures for keratoconus which can best be discussed with the ophthalmologist.

MACULAR DEGENERATION
(Senile Macular Degeneration,
Age Related Macular Degeneration)

general information—is a degenerative (age related) process involving the highly specialized central part of the retina known as the macula. The macula is responsible for detailed central vision tasks such as reading, television viewing, sewing, etc.

It is not uncommon to experience some loss of central visual function as a natural consequence of aging but some individuals suffer a much more significant and even drastic loss of central vision.

The various risk factors that may play a role in the cause of age related macular degeneration (AMD) are being intensively studied. Heredity, nutritional deficiencies, arteriosclerosis and hypertension, smoking, exposure to ultraviolet light, etc. are all suspect but further research is necessary to clearly identify the most significant factors. AMD is much more common in Caucasians and in those with light colored eyes.

There are two major types of age related macular degeneration)—the so-called atrophic (dry) variety accounting for approximately eighty percent of cases and the exudative (wet, disciform or neovascular) variety.

signs and symptoms—gradual blurring or distortion of central vision interfering with reading and sewing, etc. are the usual early symptoms in both varieties of macular degeneration. In the atrophic (dry) type, progression of visual loss is usually slow whereas the exudative or disciform (wet) type can abruptly deteriorate due to leakage of fluid or bleeding under the macula.

In many early cases, vision may not be noticeably affected and the condition is discovered on a routine medical eye examination. There is a typical appearance to the macula which alerts the ophthalmologist to the problem. Tiny yellowish deposits of degenerative material called drusen are often noted in the macular area as well as alterations in the normal structure and pigmentation of the macula.

Glasses do not correct the poor vision caused by AMD much as a new camera lens would not improve poor photographs due to damaged film.

AMD usually affects both eyes but one is often worse than the other. Many people experience only minor inconvenience from macular degeneration and are able to compensate and lead normal lives—others with the more severe forms of AMD may be incapacitated.

Although the "dry" variety outnumbers the "wet" by approximately four to one, the latter accounts for more than ninety percent of the severe visual loss due to AMD. This is due to bleeding, fluid build-up and scarring that occur in the macular area due to the presence of tiny abnormal blood vessels (neovascular membrane or net). These membranes can sometimes only be discovered by specialized photographic studies *(see fluorescein angiography, page 39)*.

While the macula (central retina) can be severely damaged by this process, the remaining ninety-five percent of the retina remains unaffected so that peripheral vision is spared and complete blindness never results from macular degeneration.

treatment—at this time only a very small number of people can benefit from early laser treatment which is limited to certain cases of the exudative or "wet" variety of AMD. Early detection of these individuals is critical. Daily inspection of an Amsler grid *(see page 46)* or a piece of graph paper is a sensitive means of detecting significant changes in the condition of the macula.

Some preliminary data is emerging regarding nutritional supplements (various vitamins and minerals) and restriction of UV light exposure with special sunglasses as possible benefits in cases of AMD. It is too early to make definitive recommendations in this regard.

MACULAR EDEMA

general information—is swelling or fluid accumulation in the macula which is the sensitive central part of the retina responsible for sharp detailed vision. There are many causes of macular edema including certain inflammations (uveitis), injuries and blood vessel disorders of the eyes.

Until recently, macular edema occurred with some frequency after cataract extraction. Fortunately, newer surgical techniques have greatly reduced the incidence of this type of macular edema. The most common vascular disorder causing macular edema is diabetic retinopathy *(see page 145)*. Advanced cases of macular edema can lead to macular cysts or macular holes.

signs and symptoms—blurred vision, especially for reading and other detailed fine vision tasks, is the cardinal symptom of macular edema. Peripheral vision is usually normal unless there are additional abnormalities in other parts of the retina or optic nerve.

treatment—is directed at the underlying cause. Diabetic macular edema can often be treated by laser photocoagulation. Inflammatory (uveitic) macular edema is treated with cortisone-containing medications. Post-cataract macular edema often does not respond well to treatment after it is well established but there is evidence that pretreatment with nonsteroidal anti-inflammatory agents may further reduce the incidence of this form of macular edema.

MACULAR GLIOSIS
(Macular Pucker, Preretinal Macular Fibrosis, Cellophane Maculopathy, Surface Wrinkling Retinopathy)

general information—is a distortion of the macula *(see page 5)* due to the development of a fibrous ("scar tissue") membrane on its surface. There are many possible underlying causes including, retinal detachment *(see page 193)*, inflammations, injuries, following laser and cryo procedures on the retina *(see pages 94 and 100)*, following posterior vitreous detachment *(see page 205)*, etc. but this condition can also occur spontaneously without obvious cause.

signs and symptoms—most commonly include blurring or distortion of central vision which may range from mild to pronounced and may affect one or both eyes. The exact diagnosis can only be made by the ophthalmologist during a careful exam of the retina.

treatment—many cases require no treatment and may stabilize or even improve slightly without intervention. Cases due to inflammation may be aided by treatment of the underlying condition. Severe cases are sometimes treated by vitrectomy and surgical "peeling" of the membrane. This may result in marked improvement in vision but may also lead to further complications.

Most cases are simply observed and often stabilize with only mild to moderate reduction in central vision.

MIGRAINE

general information—migraine is not simply a severe headache, but a condition with many potential manifestations including some striking visual symptoms which are discussed below. Migraine results from a spasm or constriction of blood vessels supplying the brain (visual and other sensory symptoms) followed by a period of blood vessel dilation or overexpansion (headache symptoms).

There are many trigger factors (dietary, hormonal, emotional, etc.) for migraine attacks. A positive family history of migraine and a past personal history of childhood motion sickness are not uncommon.

signs and symptoms—*classic migraine* involves a visual prodrome of flashing lights, jagged or shimmering lines or partial loss of vision off to one side followed by a severe headache typically on the side opposite the visual symptoms. The headache often lasts several hours and is relieved eventually by lying quietly in a darkened room. *Common migraine* is a variety without the visual prodrome and is often generalized rather than one-sided. Nausea and vomiting may also occur in the more severe cases. *Ophthalmic migraine* refers to episodes of the visual phenomena described above without a headache.

There are other significant causes of these visual symptoms (light flashes, jagged lines, etc.)—the proper diagnosis can only be made by an ophthalmologist or other qualified physician. *Ophthalmoplegic migraine* is a rare variety usually seen in children which can result in the paralysis of eye muscles.

treatment—preventive measures are important in reducing the frequency and severity of migraine episodes. Once specific trigger factors have been determined for an individual (e.g., foods such as chocolates, certain cheeses, animal fats etc.; chemicals, tobacco smoke; emotional factors, etc.) avoidance of these stimuli can result in an improvement.

The further management of migraine can be a challenging task best suited to a medical doctor (internist or neurologist) with a special interest and training in the treatment of headaches.

MYOPIA (Nearsightedness)

general information—is one of the refractive errors of the eye due to an excessive curvature of the cornea, an elongated eye or both *(see page 56)*.

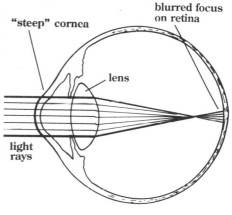

Objects at close range are seen more clearly than those farther away. The degree of myopia can vary widely as can its age of onset and rate of progression. Most nearsighted people, however, develop symptoms by age eight or nine and progress over the next several years often stabilizing by the late teens or early twenties.

Heredity appears to be the major determining factor of myopia. There is controversy regarding excessive reading and other close work as possible aggravating factors.

Myopia can also be a predisposition to retinal tears and detachments and macular disease in some individuals.

signs and symptoms—blurred vision at a distance is the primary symptom. Both eyes are usually involved but one may be significantly worse than the other. Vision tends to be worse in dim illumination and difficulty with night driving is a very common complaint.

treatment—mild, symmetrical myopia in children often requires nothing more than moving the child closer to the front of the classroom. Glasses usually become necessary for distance tasks as vision worsens to the 20/40 level or so, when symptoms require it, or when the myopia is very unequal in the two eyes.

Contact lenses can be fit, if desired, when the individual has a reasonably stable degree of myopia and is capable of handling the responsibility. Repeat exams are recommended to keep pace with the changes in prescription strength.

Radial keratotomy is a surgical procedure wherein multiple tiny slits are made in the cornea to flatten its curvature. Results have recently been very favorable and further refinements in this area are expected especially with the emerging excimer laser technology.

NEARSIGHTEDNESS *(see Myopia, page 179)*

NIGHT BLINDNESS

general information—night blindness is not actually a separate disease but rather a symptom which may be due to various other disorders.

Many nearsighted individuals experience significant difficulties seeing at night but this is considered more a "variant of normal" than a pathologic condition. Various inherited disorders including retinitis pigmentosa *(see page 196)* and its variants and congenital stationary night blindness are causes of true pathologic night blindness. Optic nerve disorders and vitamin A deficiencies can also cause night blindness.

signs and symptoms—obviously, even the perfectly normal human eye is not as well suited to vision in dim illumination as in daylight.

When performance in dim illumination on specific standardized tests is below normal the patient can be said to be more or less "night blind" but must be further evaluated to determine the specific cause.

treatment—is directed at the underlying cause. Vitamin deficiency cases can be treated as can some optic nerve problems whereas inherited "night blinding" disorders cannot.

NYSTAGMUS

general information—is an involuntary oscillation, shaking or "jiggling" of the eyes. There are many different classifications based on the type of the nystagmus and any associated underlying cause.

The more common varieties of nystagmus result from congenital and neurologic abnormalities as well as from some drugs acting on the central nervous system. Bilateral, severe abnormalities of the corneas, lenses, retinas or optic nerves can cause serious visual loss with associated congenital nystagmus.

Nystagmus noted only at the extreme points of horizontal gaze is basically a normal physiologic phenomenon ("end-point nystagmus").

signs and symptoms—include reduced vision in cases of congenital nystagmus and "jiggling" or "shaking" vision (oscillopsia) in acquired forms.

Obvious cases of marked nystagmus are easily noticed by the casual observer but some subtle forms are only discovered in the course of a careful eye exam. The shaking movements of the eyes can be side to side, up and down, diagonal or occur in various combinations as well as rarer "see-saw" and bobbing patterns. etc.

treatment—most important is the classification of the type of nystagmus present and investigation for any underlying causes such as neurologic disorders (tumors, multiple sclerosis, etc..). Any abnormalities discovered are treated by the appropriate specialists.

Some patients with congenital nystagmus can benefit from surgery on the extraocular muscles to rotate the eyes into a position where the nystagmus is less marked or absent ("null position").

OPHTHALMIA NEONATORUM
general information—refers to a potentially severe infection of an infant's eyes within the first month of life. The term was previously associated specifically with gonorrhea of the eyes which can be contracted from the infected mother during passage through the birth canal. Generally, the term *ophthalmia neonatorum* represents any of a number of infections or inflammations of the newborn's eyes.

signs and symptoms—depending on the nature and severity of a given case, ophthalmia neonatorum may range from a relatively mild inflammation to a severe potentially blinding infection with profuse discharge.

treatment—is directed at the specific causitive organism isolated by laboratory tests and cultures and usually includes potent antibiotic medications, lid hygiene and extreme caution to avoid spread of serious infections.

OPTIC ATROPHY

general information—is a destruction of optic nerve fibers which normally transmit visual impulses from the eye to the brain. This can occur on a hereditary basis, from various neurologic disorders (multiple sclerosis, optic neuritis, optic neuropathy, etc.), from vascular occlusions, glaucoma and a number of other rarer causes. The degree of optic atrophy varies with the underlying cause and the condition may affect one or both eyes.

signs and symptoms—minimal optic atrophy may cause no symptoms and be very difficult to detect on examination. More advanced optic atrophy may cause blurred, "gray" or "dim" vision or areas of partial vision loss. Very advanced optic atrophy can cause profound or even total loss of vision.

treatment—there is no treatment for optic atrophy other than efforts at limiting the progression of the underlying cause.

OPTIC NEURITIS

general information—is an inflammation of the optic nerve and may take the form of "retrobulbar neuritis" (affecting the nerve behind the eye) or "papillitis" (affecting the nerve head within the eye). In many cases of isolated optic neuritis, no specific cause for the inflammation is discovered. Possible causes in some cases include multiple sclerosis, lupus, sarcoidosis, tuberculosis and syphilis. The most commonly affected ages range form the midteens to the early forties.

signs and symptoms: rather sudden onset of decreased vision in one eye ranging from "dim vision" or patchy loss of vision to virtually total loss of light perception. The vision loss may develop over hours or days and, in cases of retrobulbar neuritis, is often accompanied by pain behind the eye especially on movement of the eye.

The proper diagnosis can only be made by the ophthalmologist or other qualified physician in the course of a thorough eye examination. Vision is usually reduced on the eye chart as well as on specialized "side vision" tests. Color vision is also often affected and there is a characteristic, abnormal pupillary reaction.

Special laboratory and X-ray tests may be performed at the discretion of the ophthalmologist to determine if there is a specific underlying disorder causing the optic neuritis. Neurologic consultation may also be advisable.

treatment—most cases of optic neuritis spontaneously improve with return of normal or near normal vision occurring within weeks to months. Cases of optic neuritis due to sarcoidosis or lupus usually require treatment with oral steroids ("cortisone").

The use of steroids in most other cases is currently not recommended. Although recovery seems to be quicker (in these nonspecific cases) with treatment there is evidence that the final outcome may not be any different with treatment and in fact, may be worse in some cases. The management of each individual is, of course, dependent on the specifics of the case.

Some degree of optic atrophy (destruction of optic nerve tissue) usually results but may not be significant or noticeable to the affected individual. The ophthalmologist can often detect the subtle changes.

OPTIC NEUROPATHY

general information—is a general term for various diseases or disorders of the optic nerve. Optic neuritis *(see page 182)* and papilledema *(see page 185)* are usually considered separately. The most common form of optic neuropathy is *ischemic optic neuropathy* which is due to a disturbance in the normal blood supply of the optic nerve. *Toxic optic neuropathy* refers to optic nerve damage from a number of different chemicals or drugs (e.g., alcohol, wood alcohol, lead poisoning, some antibiotics, digitalis, etc.). *Compressive optic neuropathy* results from pressure on the optic nerve from a tumor or other growth. *Infiltrative optic neuropathy* is rare and can result from infiltration of the nerve by tumor cells or noncancerous infiltration (e.g., sarcoidosis).

Ischemic optic neuropathy is a potentially disastrous disorder of the optic nerve which results from a disturbance in the normal circulation to the nerve. A particularly threatening form of ischemic optic neuopathy can occur in patients with temporal arteritis (giant cell arteritis, cranial arteritis) which affects the elderly.

Vision can be lost in both eyes without prompt and adequate treatment. Diabetes, hypertension, arteriosclerosis and various collagen vascular diseases can also cause ischemic optic neuropathy.

signs and symptoms—ischemic optic neuropathy usually begins suddenly with painless loss of vision in one eye which may range in degree from slight to profound and total. Partial loss of vision is often in the form of an "altitudinal defect" where the

ENCYCLOPEDIA

lower half of vision seems to be "missing". There are character-istic findings on eye examination and only an ophthalmologist or other qualified physician can make a definitive diagnosis.

Involvement of the second eye may occur especially in cases of temporal arteritis. A blood test called a "sed rate" is invaluable in diagnosing temporal arteritis and monitoring the response to treatment. A temporal artery biopsy is also sometimes per-formed to confirm the diagnosis of temporal arteritis.

treatment—ischemic optic neuropathy due to temporal arteritis requires immediate high dose steroid ("cortisone") treatment which is usually continued for a year or more. Cases due to col-lagen vascular diseases such as lupus also require cortisone treatment. Steroids have also been used very successfully in cases due to diabetes but the blood sugar must be watched closely while on medication.

The use of cortisone in cases due to arteriosclerosis is much more controversial but studies seem to indicate a beneficial re-sponse if used in adequate doses at an early stage.

ORBITAL CELLULITIS

general information—is an infection of the orbit (socket) of the eye. This can be "preseptal", involving the lids and soft tis-sues about the eye or "deep orbital", involving the main part of the orbit containing the eye and its many nerves and muscles.

Orbital cellulitis can follow an injury to the lids and orbit or can result form spread of infection from the adjacent sinuses. Ep-isodes can vary from a mild, temporary condition to a severe vi-sion and even life-threatening infection.

signs and symptoms—preseptal orbital cellulitis is character-ized by redness, tenderness and often severe swelling of the lids on one side. Deep orbital cellulitis causes the same appearance but additionally is associated with limitation of movement of the eye and may also cause significant loss of vision due to optic nerve compression. Patients with deep orbital cellulitis are also often ill with fever and eye pain.

treatment—preseptal orbital cellulitis can usually be managed on an out-patient basis with oral antibiotics. Drainage of the lid abscess is sometimes required.

More severe cases and all patients with deep orbital cellulitis require hospitalization and intravenous antibiotics. Orbital and sinus drainage procedures are sometimes necessary. Neglect of a case of deep orbital cellulitis can lead to blindness, spread of the infection to the brain and death.

PAPILLEDEMA

general information—is a noninflammatory swelling of both optic nerves due to increased pressure within the skull from a brain tumor or other space occupying lesion. A condition known as pseudotumor cerebri (or benign intracranial hypertension) can also lead to papilledema. Pseudotumor cerebri is a disorder seen usually in young, overweight females which may be precipitated by certain antibiotics and vitamin preparations. Severe systemic hypertension (high blood pressure) can also cause papilledema.

Longstanding papilledema can result in destruction of optic nerve tissue and profound loss of vision.

signs and symptoms—headaches due to the underlying cause of the papilledema are common and may be severe. "Transient obscurations of vision" (momentary losses of sight) are also sometimes noted.

The diagnosis of papilledema can only be made by an ophthalmologist or other qualified medical doctor and should always prompt an investigation as to the underlying cause. Internal medical, neurologic and radiologic consultations are usually necessary.

treatment—is directed at the underlying cause. Neurosurgery may be necessary for removal of a brain tumor. Medicines to reduce the increased intracranial pressure in pseudotumor cerebri are usually successful but a "shunt" procedure is sometimes performed to relieve pressure on the brain.

Measures to lower blood pressure are taken in cases of hypertension-induced papilledema. Some desperate cases where the optic nerve function is seriously threatened may require a surgical procedure to slit the optic nerve sheath directly reducing the pressure on the nerve.

PINGUECULA

general information—is a common, benign degenerative tissue growth on the surface of the conjunctiva.

signs and symptoms—a small yellowish mass is usually noted covering the white of the eye near the cornea on the nasal side. Occasionally this may be pink or red due to inflammation.

treatment—no treatment is necessary unless very obvious in which case cosmetic excision may be indicated. Inflamed pingueculae usually respond well to decongestant drops.

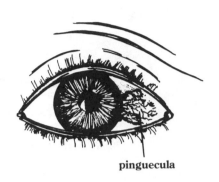

pinguecula

PRESBYOPIA

general information—is the natural weakening of the close range focus power of the eye with age due to a gradual stiffening of the crystalline lens *(see also page 57)*.

"flexible", youthful lens– focuses nearby objects on retina

Presbyopia

"stiff", presbyopic lens–
light from nearby objects focuses behind retina

signs and symptoms—difficulty with comfortable, clear focus at close range usually beginning around age forty and slowly worsening over the next three decades. Unless there is a coexisting refractive error, distance vision remains unaffected. Nearsighted individuals experience presbyopia at a later age than normal whereas farsighted people experience it earlier.

treatment—eye glasses are usually prescribed in the form of single vision reading glasses or bifocals *(see page 57)*. Bifocal contact lenses require further refinement for widespread use.

PROLIFERATIVE VITREORETINOPATHY (PVR)
Massive Vitreous Retraction (MVR)
Massive Preretinal Proliferation

general information—the terms above are various designations for a serious, vision threatening condition that can result after retinal break formation. Specialized supporting and connective tissue cells can begin to grow across the inside and outside surface of the retina eventually leading to shrinkage and contraction of the tissue with resultant traction retinal detachment.

PVR can also occur subsequent to repair of a retinal detachment.

signs and symptoms—partial or complete loss of vision may be the presenting symptoms but the specific diagnosis can only be made by the ophthalmologist. A dilated examination of the retina, usually by indirect ophthalmoscopy *(see page 36)* is necessary to visualize the entirety of the retina.

treatment— combinations of vitrectomy, scleral buckling and other advanced procedures (gas/fluid exchanges and vitreous replacement, etc.) may be necessary to salvage an eye with PVR.

Anatomic reattachment of the retina can be achieved in most cases but the visual prognosis is more guarded.

PROPTOSIS *(See Exophthalmos, page 159.)*

PSEUDOSTRABISMUS

general information—refers to the *illusion* of strabismus (misalignment of the eyes) usually due to certain anatomic facial features commonly seen in infants. Folds of skin extending from the upper lids to the lower lids near the bridge of the nose (epicanthal folds) can obscure visualization of the sclera (white of the eye) creating the illusion of crossing eyes. Infants also commonly have a broad, flat nasal bridge contributing to the appearance of crossing eyes. A large percentage of children referred to ophthalmologists for possible esotropia (crossed eyes) are, in fact, straight (pseudostrabismic). Parents, grandparents, relatives and friends as well as other physicians commonly mistake pseudostrabismus for true misalignments.

signs and symptoms—
observer's impression of eyes crossing usually in an infant or young child especially when the child is looking to one side. A penlight or other small point light source helps to differentiate true from pseudostrabismus. Shining the light directly at the child's eyes creates corneal light reflections which, if centered in both pupils, indicates that the eyes are probably straight. If the reflection is centered in one

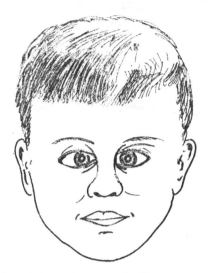

pupil and displaced to one side of the other, a misalignment of the eyes is probably present. This test and other more definitive tests, are subject to the experienced ophthalmologist's interpretation.

Many children have subtle or intermittent misalignments which require careful professional evaluation for a definitive diagnosis.

treatment—No treatment is indicated for psuedostrabismus since this simply represents the *illusion* of an ocular misalignment and is outgrown as the facial anatomy develops and matures. It is obviously important, however, for the ophthalmologist to distinguish between true and pseudostrabismus. A complete medical eye examination should be scheduled without delay once strabismus is suspected.

PTERYGIUM

general information—is a degenerative tissue growth on the surface of the conjunctiva extending on to the cornea often in the shape of a triangle with the apex pointing toward the cornea. The cause is unknown but pterygia are more commonly seen in people exposed to to the elements (sun, wind, dust, etc.).

signs and symptoms—yellowish-white triangular shaped mass extending from the conjunctiva onto the cornea for a variable distance usually located on the nasal side of the eye. The condition usually occurs on both eyes though often quite asymmetrically. Inflamed pterygia often appear pink or red and may cause considerable ocular irritation. Vision may be affected if the pterygium encroaches toward the center of the cornea or causes astigmatism by distorting the normal corneal curvature.

treatment—many pterygia require no treatment and may remain quite stable. Occasionally, significant inflammation and active growth may occur necessi-

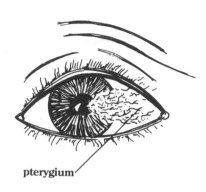

pterygium

tating surgical excision. Less severe inflammation may be successfully treated with decongestant or steroid ("cortisone") eye drops under medical supervision. Recurrences after excision are common and may be prevented by various means. The possibility of a superficial ocular cancer mimicking a pterygium must always be kept in mind.

PTOSIS (Blepharoptosis)
    general information—is the term for drooping of the lid (usually refers to upper lid). This can occur from neurologic (e.g., third nerve palsy), neuromuscular (e.g., myasthenia gravis), or mechanical (e.g., lid swelling) causes as well as from injuries or aging changes. Ptosis can also occur following routine intraocular surgery (e.g., cataract surgery).

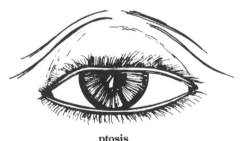

ptosis
(drooping upper eye lid)

Very small degrees of ptosis can sometimes be considered variations of normal.

signs and symptoms—drooping of the upper lid may be very subtle and only noted on a medical eye examination or be total with complete involuntary closure of the eye. Ptosis may affect one or both eyes and can be very asymmetrical depending on the underlying cause. Some cases may even be episodic or intermittent as in myasthenia gravis.

treatment—neurologic and neuromuscular cases often either improve spontaneously or respond to treatment of the underlying cause. Similarly, cases due to swelling of the lid improve with treatment of the condition that caused the swelling. Cases due to injury and any other case of ptosis that does not spontaneously improve or respond to treatment of the underlying cause can be considered for surgical correction. In neurologic cases a six month waiting period should elapse before surgery *(see page 101)*.

RECURRENT CORNEAL EROSION
general information—is a recurring erosion or sloughing of the protective skin (epithelium) of the cornea. Most recurrent erosions are preceded by an abrasion injury of the cornea usually by a sharp glancing object such as a fingernail, tree branch or mascara brush, etc. In some cases, a definite predisposing injury can not be recalled—other cases result from an underlying corneal dystrophy *(see page 140)*.

Multiple episodes of recurrent erosion occur at varying intervals. This is thought to occur because of faulty adhesions or bonds between the skin cells and the underlying tissue resulting from the preceding injury or dystrophy. The condition may affect one or both eyes.

signs and symptoms—recurring episodes of pain (often severe) in the eye frequently occurring upon arising. Tearing, light sensitivity and blurred vision often accompany the pain. An episode may last from a few hours to days.

treatment—topical lubricants and concentrated salt solutions as well as antibiotic drops are usually used to treat recurrences. Severe or very persistent cases are sometimes treated with a "bandage soft contact lens" or collagen corneal shield. Newer procedures including "corneal puncture" and even excimer laser ablation have been used successfully for advanced cases.

RETINAL ARTERY OCCLUSION
general information—the retinal arteries (arterioles) supply blood to the retina and consist of a complex branching network of vessels extending from the central retinal artery which emerges from the optic nerve at the back of the eye *(see pages 5 and*

14). Blockages in these vessels may occur at various points due to atherosclerosis, clots, emboli (cholesterol, calcium, fat, etc.) originating from a distant site and lodging in the vessel), spasm, inflammation, etc.

Central retinal artery occlusions (CRAOs) result from a blockage in the main artery at the level of the optic nerve and usually lead to severe and permanent loss of vision in the affected eye. Branch retinal artery occlusions (BRAOs) usually occur at some distance from the optic nerve at branching sites and may or may not cause significant loss of vision depending on the part of the retina involved.

signs and symptoms—sudden, painless loss of vision in one eye (vision may go completely black) characterizes a central retinal artery occlusion. Branch retinal artery occlusions may go unnoticed if the macular (central retinal) blood supply is not affected. Significant branch retinal artery occlusions may manifest themselves as partial loss of the field of vision. Retinal artery occlusions can only be properly diagnosed by an ophthalmologist or other qualified medical doctor.

treatment—lowering the intraocular fluid pressure by various means can help to restore blood flow within the retinal vessels and will occasionally reverse the damage done by a retinal artery occlusion. This should always be attempted but must be carried out very soon after the occlusion if any degree of success is to be expected.

It is very important to discover and treat any significant underlying medical conditions such as hypertension, carotid artery disease, cardiac valvular disease, diabetes, temporal arteritis, etc.

RETINAL BREAKS (Retinal Holes, Retinal Tears)

general information—"retinal break" is the general term for any disruption in the retina and can take the form of a round hole or a tear which is often horseshoe-shaped. High degrees of myopia (nearsightedness) definitely predispose an eye to develop retinal breaks. Injuries (especially in boxers, for example) and a positive family history are other predisposing factors. There is also an increased incidence of retinal tears and detachment following cataract surgery. This complication has become much less frequent with recent advances in cataract surgery.

Some retinal breaks develop from thinned areas at the edge of the retina (lattice retinal degeneration); others develop as a result of traction of the vitreous gel on the retina. Some severe diabetics develop abnormal scar tissue in the vitreous which can contract causing retinal tears and detachments.

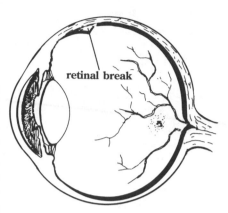

The major significance of retinal breaks is their potential for leading to a retinal detachment *(see page 193)*. Fluid passes through the break and accumulates beneath the retina eventually separating the retina from the underlying layers of the eye.

signs and symptoms—retinal breaks (especially small, round degenerative holes) may develop with no symptoms and only be discovered as part of a thorough (dilated) examination of the peripheral retina. Horseshoe shaped tears resulting from vitreoretinal traction are often accompanied by "flashes and floaters". The "flashes" may resemble lightning or electric sparks and may only be noticed at night or in a darkened room. "Floaters" may take the form of spots, flies, cobwebs, or strings, etc. floating in the field of vision.

Occasionally, a retinal tear is associated with a torn blood vessel in the retina which can bleed into the vitreous and cause more profound visual symptoms.

Depending on the amount of blood, a cloud over part of the vision, smoky vision, or even loss of vision may result. If a retinal detachment closely follows the development of a retinal tear, a veil or shade may seem to be drawing across the field of vision and, if the macula becomes detached, central vision may be lost.

treatment—some retinal breaks can simply be observed over time by the ophthalmologist. There are various characteristics of retinal breaks that may make them more or less threatening for the development of retinal detachment. Depending on the type and location of the break, laser "retinopexy" may be indicated to wall off the break from the surrounding retina and prevent the passage of fluid under the retina. Some breaks require freezing ("cryopexy") and still others may need a surgical procedure to prevent or limit retinal detachment. The specific form of treatment depends on the individual circumstances and the preference of the ophthalmic surgeon *(see pages 94 and 100)*.

RETINAL DETACHMENT

general information—is a separation of the retina (nerve cell layer) from the outer layers of the eye *(see page 5)*. The detachment may be small, localized and insignificant or involve the entire retina resulting in blindness if not quickly and properly treated.

Nearsighted individuals are more commonly affected due to the thinning of the retina often seen in myopic eyes. Holes or tears can develop in the thinned retina through which fluid passes to separate the retina from the adjacent layers of the eye.

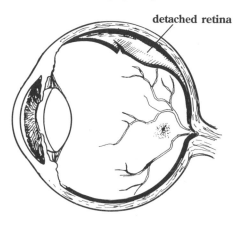

detached retina

Injuries to the head or eyes often precipitate the detachment. The vitreous (gel fluid within the eye) also plays a significant role in retinal detachment by tugging on the underlying retina ("vitreous traction"). Cataract surgery can also be a precipitating factor but this is rarer now with modern cataract surgical techniques. A positive family history of retinal detachment is another risk factor.

Detachment of the retina can also occur without a preexisting break in the retina. In these instances fluid accumulates underneath the retina from inflammation or other causes. Scarring within the eye (especially in severe diabetic retinopathy) can also lead to retinal detachment. Most cases of retinal detachment, however, are due to retinal holes or tears (rhegmatogenous retinal detachment).

signs and symptoms—classically, a retinal detachment is heralded by "flashes and floaters". The sudden awareness of bright flashing light spots or streaks and dark moving specks is due to vitreous traction on the retina (light flashes) and solid vitreous material, a plug of retinal tissue, or blood (floaters). "Flashes and floaters" can also commonly occur from simple vitreous alterations, as well as other causes, without retinal tear or detachment. Only a thorough dilated examination of the retina by a qualified ophthalmologist can determine the cause of the symptoms.

Retinal detachments can also proceed unnoticed until a large quadrant or section of the retina is detached, at which time the individual may note that part of their vision was "missing"—this may be above, below or off to one side. Some describe this as a veil, curtain or shade, covering a part of the vision.

treatment—once the retina has actually detached it must be surgically reattached. Traditionally, this has meant a "scleral buckling" procedure where a silicone material is sutured to the sclera (white of the eye) behind the lids indenting the globe inward. Freezing applications are applied to create a controlled degree of inflammation through the sclera which, in turn, helps bind the retina to the overlying choroid and sclera *(see page 94)*.

Many newer techniques are being used and developed for the treatment of some detachments including intraocular gas injections and balloon retinopexy where a tiny inflatable balloon is sutured to the sclera to serve the same purpose as the silicone "buckle" and is deflated and removed after the retina has reattached.

Some small very localized detachments can simply be delimited with laser or freezing treatment.

The success rate for "anatomic" reattachment of the retina is quite high but, if the macula (sensitive central portion of the retina) has been detached for any length of time, the "functional" success of the surgery may be poor with regard to maintenance of good central vision.

Complicated detachments (giant retinal breaks and traction detachments, etc.) may require multiple procedures including vitrectomy (removal of vitreous) and usually have less favorable prognoses.

RETINAL VEIN OCCLUSION

general information—the retinal veins (venous drainage system) return blood from the retina to the general circulation. There is an extensive branching network of veins throughout the retina *(see page 14)*. Blockages may occur at various points in this system resulting in spillage of blood into the surrounding retina and corresponding loss of vision. These blockages are usually the result of blood vessel damage from hypertension or diabetes, spasm of the blood vessels, inflammatory reactions in the vessels or sludging of blood flow due to various rare blood conditions.

Central retinal vein occlusions (CRVOs) occur at a point where all the branch veins empty into a common vessel at the level of the optic nerve and may be partial (venous stasis retinopathy) or complete (hemorrhagic CRVO).

Branch Retinal Vein Occlusions (BRVOs) occur along one of the branch veins, usually at a point where one of the retinal arteries crosses over the vein causing a "crimp" in the vein. BRVO is one of the most common causes of visual loss from retinal blood vessel disease. Retinal vein occlusions usually occur in an older population with a peak incidence in the sixties although younger people can be affected particularly when inflammations of the veins are at fault. Men are more commonly affected than women.

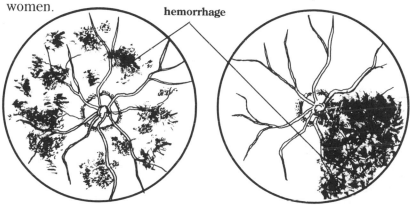

hemorrhage

central retina vein occlusion   branch retinal vein occlusion

signs and symptoms—sudden, painless loss of vision in one eye characterizes a central retinal vein occlusion. Branch retinal vein occlusions may be much less obvious and even unnoticed if one of the less important branches is affected. If a branch draining the macula (center of the retina) is involved, vision loss may be quite marked and may often take the form of a wedge shaped area of decreased or lost vision.

The amount of retinal swelling, bleeding and nerve cell damage determine the degree of vision loss and the prognosis for recovery. Retinal vein occlusions can only be properly diagnosed by an ophthalmologist or other qualified medical doctor.

treatment—careful examination of the retina, including photography and fluorescein angiography are essential to the best management of retinal vein occlusions. Fluorescein angiography elucidates the fine details of retinal blood flow and is the best means of detecting early complications from the occlusion. Laser treatment has been shown to be effective both in the limitation of damage from some vein occlusions and in the prevention of complications (i.e., new blood vessel formation or neovascularization with potential bleeding and secondary glaucoma).

It is, of course, also necessary to treat any underlying medical problems such as hypertension, diabetes and blood diseases as well as to control coexisting glaucoma.

Despite all attempts, however, a significant number of retinal vein occlusions result in profound loss of vision. Fortunately, only one eye is usually involved.

RETINITIS PIGMENTOSA

general information—is a progressive degenerative disorder of the retina which can cause profound loss of vision. Various hereditary patterns (dominant, recessive, sex linked) have been reported but sporadic cases are the most common.

signs and symptoms—include decreased night vision and decreased peripheral vision starting in the first or second decade of life (later in the dominantly inherited variety). Marked loss of vision occurs over many years but may develop very slowly. The diagnosis is made by a careful ophthalmologic exam although special testing (electroretinogram, "ERG") may be necessary in questionable cases. The ERG is also useful in monitoring the progression of the disease and to establish genetic patterns.

treatment—there is no known effective treatment for retinitis pigmentosa at this time.

RETROLENTAL FIBROPLASIA (RLF)
RETINOPATHY OF PREMATURITY (ROP)

general information—both terms describe a retinal blood vessel disorder which can occur in low birth weight premature infants. Much more commonly seen in the 1950s before the causes were elucidated, RLF is rarely encountered today.

Excess oxygen administration to high risk premature infants is thought to cause an obliteration of the tiny developing blood vessels at the edge of the retina. Neovascularization, or abnormal blood vessel development may then occur leading to bleeding, scar tissue formation and retinal detachment. Advanced cases can lead to total loss of vision.

Modern day neonatal intensive care units are acutely aware of the need for careful oxygen monitoring and early ophthalmological consultations.

signs and symptoms—only a very careful dilated retinal examination by a qualified ophthalmologist can detect the early signs of RLF. This should normally be performed upon discharge from the hospital or by two months of age.

treatment—the best treatment for RLF is prevention. Laser, cryo and scleral buckling procedures have been performed where indicated, with some degree of success. There is no known medical treatment for RLF.

Mild cases often regress spontaneously with good visual recovery whereas severe advanced cases may be resistant to all forms of treatment and may result in profound loss of vision.

Follow up examinations throughout life are necessary for children discovered to have RLF in order to detect and treat any of the late complications of the disease.

SCLERITIS

general information—is an inflammation of the sclera or "white" of of the eye often associated with one of the "collagen vascular" or "connective tissue" diseases such as rheumatoid arthritis and can also occur in association with ulcerative colitis, Chron's disease, Behcet's disease, etc. Scleritis occurs more commonly in females, involves both eyes in approximately half the cases and may be chronic and recurrent. There are various subtypes classified according to the part of the eye affected and the exact nature of the inflammation.

signs and symptoms—redness of the eye (may be diffuse or more localized) with boring pain. "Nodular" scleritis may be extremely painful. "Necrotizing" scleritis may lead to thinning of the sclera and even perforation (scleromalacia perforans). The underlying colored uveal tissue may protrude through the sclera giving rise to a bluish appearance of the eye. The course of scleritis is quite variable from person to person.

treatment—An investigation for a specific underlying medical disorder should be undertaken so treatment may be instituted if possible. Steroid ("cortisone") drops help to relieve symptoms. Oral steroids may become necessary in some cases. Other treatments including nonsteroidal anti-inflammatory agents such as indomethacin and immunosuppressive agents have been used. Some severe cases even require surgery to manage perforations of the eye and others progress despite all measures and are usually associated with very serious medical disease.

SECONDARY MEMBRANE
(Opacified Posterior Capsule)

general information—most cataract operations today are performed by some form of "extracapsular" technique where the skin or "capsule" of the cataract is left in place within the eye *(see page 92)* to help maintain the normal anatomy of the eye. These techniques have greatly improved the results of cataract surgery and reduced the incidence of such complications as retinal detachment and macular edema.

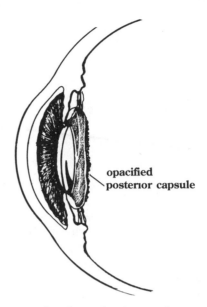

opacified
posterior capsule

The capsule can, however, become cloudy or hazy months to years after the surgery and does so in a third or so of cases. This does not represent a regrowth of the cataract but is due to a thin layer of "scar tissue" growing across the capsule.

signs and symptoms—are often similar to those caused by the original cataract, i.e., blurred or distorted vision, haziness, glare etc. developing gradually months to years after the cataract surgery.

treatment—today, the treatment is rather simple—a short painless treatment with the YAG laser (YAG laser posterior capsulotomy). Complications can and do occur in some cases (pressure elevation within the eye, retinal detachment, etc.) but this is generally a safe procedure and far easier to perform than the previously required surgical capsulotomy. Once an adequate opening is obtained, the procedure need never be repeated *(see page 98)*.

SIXTH (ABDUCENS) CRANIAL NERVE PALSY
(Lateral Rectus Palsy)

general information—is a paralysis (or "paresis" in partial cases) of the nerve which operates the outward turning muscle of the eye (lateral rectus muscle). Causes include injuries, tumors, elevated intracranial pressure, vascular insufficiency, diabetes, multiple sclerosis, and various inflammations. Sixth nerve palsies may also occur in association with other cranial nerve palsies.

signs and symptoms—double vision (horizontally separate images) results from the eyes being misaligned and is greatest when looking toward the side of the affected eye. Single binocular vision is usually present when looking to the opposite side. In a complete sixth nerve palsy the eyes usually look crossed, the affected eye turning inward.

treatment—the underlying cause of the sixth nerve palsy must, of course, be investigated and any appropriate treatment is instituted.

In the acute phases, patching of the eye to eliminate the double vision is all that is usually necessary. Prism glasses are also sometimes useful. The palsy usually spontaneously improves over weeks to months. After six months, persistent sixth nerve palsies may require eye muscle surgery. Injection of botulinum toxin into the overacting inward pulling muscle (medial rectus) has also been reported as helpful in some cases.

STRABISMUS

general information—is the general term for any misalignment of the eyes regardless of type, cause or age of onset. "Crossed eyes" (esotropia) and "wall eyes" (exotropia) are both examples of strabismus. Strabismus may be paralytic (due to a weak or paralyzed muscle) or non-paralytic (due to congenital imbalance or "focus" factors, etc.)

signs and symptoms—diagnosis is obvious enough when there is a significant, constant turn present but much more difficult with subtle, intermittent misalignments. Children with strabismus usually do not complain since they adapt quickly and suppress or ignore the vision from the deviating eye, thus avoiding double vision. Unless a turn is actually noted by a family member, teacher or health care personnel, children with strabismus and amblyopia *(see page 126)* can go undiagnosed and untreated.

Another common problem is the over diagnosis of strabismus by the same groups of people *(see pseudostrabismus, page 187)*.

treatment—depends entirely on the specific type of strabismus (see e.g., esotropia, exotropia, etc.) In general, the earlier the condition is detected and treated, the better the eventual outcome. It is critically important that any associated amblyopia is eliminated at the earliest possible age to allow for normal development of vision.

SUBCONJUNCTIVAL HEMORRHAGE

general information—is due to a broken blood vessel on the surface of the eye. Injuries, violent straining (sneezing, coughing, etc.), hypertension, certain bleeding disorders, etc. are among the possible causes. More commonly, however, a subconjunctival hemorrhage may just occur spontaneously with no underlying cause.

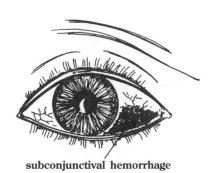

subconjunctival hemorrhage

signs and symptoms—bright red blood plates out between the sclera (white of the eye) and the conjunctiva (thin transparent skin of the eye) and can range from a small blood spot to coverage of the entire sclera.

treatment—no treatment is necessary in most cases. The blood spontaneously reabsorbs over several days with no effect on vision.

SYMPATHETIC OPHTHALMIA

general information—is a rare, potentially devastating inflammation of the eye that can occasionally develop after certain types of penetrating injuries in the *opposite* eye. Exposure of some of the internal contents of the eye form the injury initiates an immunologic process which causes inflammation in the same type of tissue in the fellow eye.

Sympathetic ophthalmia can occur, at the earliest, between one and two weeks following the injury or as long as years later.

signs and symptoms—include severe light sensitivity, difficulty focusing and eventually marked inflammation in the eye *opposite* the injured eye.

treatment—high dose cortisone treatment has been successful in managing many cases of sympathetic ophthalmia which, in the past, would have lead to blindness.

TEARING *(see Epiphora, page 152)*

TEMPORAL ARTERITIS (Giant Cell Arteritis)

general information—is an inflammatory condition involving the temporal artery (a large blood vessel on the side of the head) and its branches. Most patients are around seventy years of age and often suffer from the the generalized condition, polymyalgia rheumatica which consists of multiple joint and muscle pains, fever, fatigue and weight loss, etc.

The blood vessel inflammation can cause a blockage of the arteries supplying the eye and lead to irreversible blindness. Eye muscle paralysis with double vision can also occur. Both eyes are at risk but involvement of one usually precedes the other.

signs and symptoms—besides the generalized symptoms of polymyalgia rheumatica mentioned above, headaches, scalp tenderness along the side of the head and pain on chewing can also be noted.

Vision loss may be preceded by periods of amaurosis fugax *(see page 126)* but can also be sudden and complete due to central retinal artery occlusion or gradual in cases of anterior ischemic optic neuropathy *(see page 183)*.

More rarely, uveitis, cataract and glaucoma may occur or double vision may develop if the extraocular muscles are involved.

Blood tests (erythrocyte sedimentation rate) and temporal artery biopsy may be necessary to confirm the diagnosis.

treatment—high dose, long term cortisone treatment can sometimes reverse the damage or at least prevent a similar occurrence in the fellow eye.

THIRD (OCULOMOTOR) CRANIAL NERVE PALSY

general information—is a paralysis (or "paresis" in partial cases) of the nerve which operates most of the extraocular muscles, the internal eye muscles and the muscle responsible for raising the upper lid. This can occur on a congenital basis or, more commonly, develop later in life due to a number of underlying causes. Compression of the nerve by tumor or aneurysm, injuries, diabetes, vascular insufficiency, inflammations, and multiple sclerosis are among the possible causes. Third nerve palsies may also occur in association with other cranial nerve palsies.

signs and symptoms—a complete third nerve palsy causes the upper lid to droop (ptosis), the eye to turn outward and the pupil to be dilated. There are many cases of partial nerve involvement with sparing of one or more of the third nerve's functions.

The major symptom (if the eye is not covered by the drooping lid) is double vision due to the misalignment of the eyes. The affected eye, in a complete third nerve palsy can not turn inward, up or down and the pupil does not constrict to a light stimulus. The vision may also be blurred due to paralysis of the internal focusing muscle of the eye.

treatment—the cause of the third nerve palsy must first be determined and any appropriate treatment instituted. This may require neurologic consultation and various laboratory tests. Treatment of the actual palsy involves patching of the eye to eliminate double vision.

Depending on the underlying cause, spontaneous improvement may occur over six to nine months. If improvement is not adequate, muscle transposition surgery can be performed in an attempt to at least center the eye if not regain some of the normal movements. The ptosis can also be surgically repaired once the eye is realigned.

THYROID EYE DISEASE
general information—various disorders of the eyes may occur as a result of, or as an accompaniment to, thyroid disease. The thyroid gland which is situated in the neck is responsible for the production of certain hormones which regulate metabolism. Overaction of the thyroid gland (hyperthyroidism) speeds up the metabolism and is manifested by increased appetite, nervousness, rapid heart beat, sweating and weight loss, etc. Underaction of the thyroid gland (hypothyroidism) slows the metabolism down and is manifested by decreased appetite, lethargy, weight gain, etc.

For reasons that are still not entirely clear, the eyes can be affected especially in cases of hyperthyroidism (thyrotoxicosis, Graves' disease).The eye findings may precede the diagnosis of hyperthyroidism but may also only be noted following treatment for the thyroid condition when thyroid hormone levels in the blood are normal or low.

Women are affected more often than men and the most common age group for eye disease is between thirty and fifty. The active condition (swelling and inflammation) is usually self limited after several months but may persist for several years. Scar tissue resulting from the inflammation (e.g., in the extraocular muscles) is permanent.

signs and symptoms—any or all of the following may be noted: retraction of the upper eyelid (i.e., upper lid raised higher than normal); lid lag (i.e., upper lid does not lower normally when looking downward); irritation and foreign body sensation; redness and swelling of the conjunctiva; limitation of extraocular muscle movement in one or more directions and extraocular muscle imbalances; proptosis or exophthalmos (one or both eyes protrude outward); exposure damage to the cornea and conjunctiva from proptosis; optic nerve compression with possible loss of vision due to swelling in the orbit.

treatment—Specialized testing of the visual field (side vision), color vision testing, CT scanning, ultrasonography, and periodic complete medical eye examinations should be carried out as dictated by the specifics of a given case. Consultation with an internist and/or an endocrinologist are usually necessary.

Proptosis and exposure may simply require lubricant drops and ointments and lid taping at night. Suturing of the lids (tarsorraphy) may be necessary in some cases. Oral prednisone is sometimes indicated for severe congestion and swelling of tissues. Orbital decompression (surgical procedure to release pressure in the orbit) is occasionally necessitated in vision-threatening situations. After the active inflammatory phase, eye muscle surgery can be performed in an effort to realign the eyes.

TRICHIASIS

general information—is the condition of misdirected or "ingrown" lashes which rub against, and irritate, the eye.

signs and symptoms—foreign body sensation, irritation, redness and tearing may all occur and vary with the severity of the condition (i.e., number, type and direction of growth of the lashes). Close inspection will reveal the abnormal lashes to be the cause of the problem.

treatment—simple "epilation" or removal of lashes affords temporary relief but the lash often regrows. Electrolysis, cryosurgery (freezing) and laser are the more definitive treatments for this condition.

TUMORS *(see also eyelid lesions, page 161)*

general information—tumors of the eye (e.g., retinoblastomas, malignant melanomas, gliomas and metastatic tumors, etc.) are rare disorders. Consult your ophthalmolgist for further information.

signs and symptoms—depend on the specific tumor.

treatment—depends on the specific tumor.

UVEITIS

general information—is the general term for inflammations of the uvea or pigmented (colored) tissue of the eye. The uvea consists of the iris (visible colored part of the eye), the ciliary body which lies behind the iris and the choroid which underlies the retina in the back of the eye. Inflammations of the uvea may involve the entire uvea (panuveitis) or its parts (iris = iritis; ciliary body = cyclitis; iris and ciliary body = iridocyclitis; choroid = choroiditis and chorioretinitis).

Uveitis may be sterile or due to various forms of infection and may also be acute, chronic or chronic/recurrent. In many cases, a specific underlying cause can not be found; other cases may be due to a number of different local (ocular) or systemic (general medical) causes.

signs and symptoms—variable degrees of pain, redness, blurred vision and light sensitivity. Some chronic cases may cause little or no symptoms and only be discovered by a careful eye examination. The redness of the eye occurring in uveitis is often of a deep red to violet hue and is most pronounced near the limbus (junction of the white sclera and the clear cornea).

Discharge is not normally present, helping to distinguish uveitis from conjunctivitis, but tearing from light sensitivity may be copious. One or both eyes may be affected depending on the exact type of uveitis. The duration and severity of the uveitis is highly dependent on the underlying cause. Severe and long-standing cases can lead to complications such as cataract, glaucoma and macular edema, sometimes with profound loss of vision.

treatment—depending on the specifics of a given case, a great many laboratory tests may be performed to isolate an underlying cause for the uveitis. These may include blood tests, skin tests, urinalysis, X-rays, etc.

Most cases of uveitis require some form of steroid ("cortisone") treatment in the form of drops, injections near the eye or pills. Dilating drops (mydriatic/cycloplegics) help to relax muscle spasm within the eye and to prevent scarring of the iris to the lens. If there is a specific infectious agent responsible for the uveitis (e.g., toxoplasmosis) special therapy geared to that infection is also instituted. Treatment may need to be prolonged beyond resolution of the acute episode in many cases to prevent a flare-up or recurrence.

VITREOUS DETACHMENT
(Posterior Vitreous Detachment)

general information—the vitreous humor is a jelly-like substance filling the inside of the eyeball which gradually degenerates and liquifies with age. There are attachments of the vitreous to the retina at various points (including the macula) and to the optic nerve.

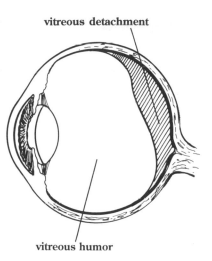

vitreous detachment

vitreous humor

As the vitreous liquifies it can detach from the macula and optic nerve ("posterior vitreous detachment" or "PVD") and cause various disturbing symptoms (see below). Posterior vitreous detachment occurs in about a quarter of people by the sixties and in up to two thirds by the eighties and is somewhat more common in women.

signs and symptoms—sudden detachment of the vitreous from the macular area usually causes the perception of "flashes and floaters". The flashes can look like lightning, or electric sparks and the floaters may resemble threads or specks . If the circular attachment to the optic nerve is separated, a large ring, circle or "C" shape may be noticed in the line of vision.

The floaters often drift across the line of vision and may be more or less noticed depending on the direction of gaze and the surrounding lighting conditions. Symptoms from a PVD may last days to weeks and should always prompt an examination by an ophthalmologist to rule out more serious consequences of vitreous detachment (retinal breaks, detachments and hemorrhages, etc.). Some people experience little or no symptoms from their vitreous detachment if it occurs smoothly with little traction on the retina.

treatment—no specific treatment is necessary for a PVD. A thorough dilated examination of the retina and vitreous should be performed by the ophthalmologist to uncover any serious associated problems. Persistent or worsening symptoms should always prompt a re-examination.

VITREOUS HEMORRHAGE

general information—is bleeding into the vitreous gel of the eye most commonly from vascular disorders of the retina such as diabetic retinopathy. Injuries and retinal tears can also result in vitreous hemorrhages.

signs and symptoms—sudden, painless loss of vision in the affected eye is the usual major symptom. Less severe vitreous hemorrhages may only cause blurred or "smoky" vision, "floaters" or "veils".

treatment—most vitreous hemorrhages reabsorb with time but may take several months. Once sufficient clearing has occurred, laser treatment (for diabetic retinopathy or other select cases) may clear up the underlying abnormality *(see page 99)*.

In some persistent cases, an operation (vitrectomy) may be necessary to evacuate the blood before retinal nerve cell damage occurs *(see page 95)*.

APPENDIX

REFERENCES FOR FURTHER READING

ontact Lens Handbook. James R. Lee, M.D.
Published by W.B. Saunders Co., Philadelphia, PA 19105 1986

ataracts: The Complete Guide from Diagnosis to Recovery for Patient and Family.
lius Schulman, M.D.
Published by AARP Washington, D.C., Scott Forsman and Co., Glenview, IL 1985

Layman's Guide to Cataract Surgery. William Maloney, M.D.
Published by Lasenda Publishers, Fallbrook, CA 92028 1986

ataracts: What You Must Know About Them. Charles D. Kelman, M.D.
Published by The Crown Publishing Group (large print edition published by G.K. Hall & Co.)

acular Degeneration. Howard Schatz, M.D. and H. Richard MacDonald, M.D.
Published by Retina Research Fund, St. Mary's Hospital, PO Box 590238, San Francisco, CA 94159 1987

w Vision: What You Can Do To Preserve–and Even Enhance–Your Useable yesight. Helen Neal
Published by Simon and Schuster, Inc., 1230 Avenue of the Americas, New York, NY 10020 1987

merican Foundation for the Blind/Directory of Agencies, Serving the visually ndicapped in the U.S. (21st ed.)
Published by American Foundation for the Blind, 15 West 16th Street. New York, NY 10011 1981

ternational Catalog: Aids and Appliances for Blind and Visually Impaired ersons.
Published by American Foundation for the Blind, 15 West 16th Street. New York, NY 10011 1981

ecommended Aids for the Partially Sighted. Louise L. Sloan, Ph. D.
Published by National Society for the Prevention of Blindness, 79 Madison Avenue, New York, NY 10016

ote: Additional literature can be obtained through:

The American Academy of Ophthalmology
P.O. Box 7024
San Francisco, CA 94120

American Diabetes Association
1660 Duke Street
Alexandria, VA 22314
(800) 232-3472

APPENDIX

RESOURCES

Affiliated Leadership League Of And For
The Blind Of America
879 Park Avenue
Baltimore, MD 21201
301-752-4230

American Academy of Ophthalmology
P.O. Box 7024
San Francisco, CA 94120

American Association For Pediatric
Ophthalmology And Strabismus
c/o Arthur Rosenblum, M.D.
Jules Stein Eye Institute
UCLA Medical Center
Los Angeles, CA 90024

American Association Of Workers For
the Blind, Inc.
1511 K Street NW
Washington, DC 20005
202-347-1559

American Bible Society
1865 Broadway
New York, NY 10023
212-581-7400

American Diabetes Association
1660 Duke Street
Alexandria, VA 22314
703-549-1500

American Intraocular Implant Society
P.O. Box 3140
Santa Monica, CA 90403

American Printing House For The Blind
1839 Frankfort Avenue
Louisville, KY 40206
502-895-2405

American Society of Catartact and
Refractive Surgery
American Society of Ophthalmic
Administrators (ASCRS/ASOA)
3702 Pender Drive, Suite 250
Fairfax, VA 22030
703-591-2220

Association For Research And Vision In
Ophthalmology
C-1002 Wykagyl Street
New Rochelle, NY 10804

Association For Macular Disease
210 E. 64th Street
New York, NY 10021

Association For Education Of The
Visually Handicapped
919 Walnut Street
7th Floor
Philadelphia, PA 19107
215-923-7555

Bureau For The Blind And Visually
Handicapped
330 C Street SW
Washington DC
202-245-0918

Benign Essential Blepharospasm
Research Foundation
755 Howell Street
Beaumont, TX 77706
713-892-1339

Better Vision Institute
230 Park Avenue
New York, NY 10169
212-682-1731

CLAO
Contact Lens Association of
Ophthalmologists
2620 Jena Street
New Orleans, LA 70115
504-891-5442

Eye Bank Association Of America
6560 Fannin Street
Houston, TX 77030
713-797-9270

Eye Research Institute Of The Retina
Foundation
20 Stanford Street
Boston, MA 02144
617-742-3140

Fight For Sight, Inc.
National Council To Combat Blindness
139 E. 57th Street
New York, NY 10022
212-751-1118

Foundation for Children With Learning
Disabilities
P.O. Box 2929
Grand Central Station
New York, NY 10163

Foundation For Glaucoma Research
490 Post Street
Suite 1101
San Francisco, CA 94102

Foundation For Education And
Research In Vision
1016 La Poseda
Suite 174
Austin, TX 78752

Glaucoma Society Of The International
Congress Of Ophthalmology
c/o John Hethrington, M.D.
374 Parnassus
Suite 210
San Francisco, CA 94143

Horizons For The Blind
7001 N. Clark Street
Chicago, IL 60626
312-973-7600

Industrial Home For The Blind
57 Willoughby Street
Brooklyn, NY 11201

Information For The Partially Sighted
9012 Old Georgetown Road
Bethesda, MD 20814
301-493-6300

International Strabismological
Association
Wills Eye Hospital
9th and Walnut Streets
Philadelphia, PA 19107

International Glaucoma Congress
American Medical Association
535 N. Dearborn Street
Chicago, IL 60610

International Myopia Prevention
Association
R.D. 5, Box 171
Ligonier, PA 15658

International Association Of Ocular
Surgeons
American Medical Association
535 N. Dearborn Street
Chicago, IL 60610

International Association Of Lions Clubs
300 22nd Street
Oak Brook, IL 60570
312-986-1700

Jules Stein Eye Institute
UCLA Center for Health Services
800 Westwood Plaza
Los Angeles, CA 90024
213-825-5051

Keratorefractive Society
P.O. Box 145
Denison, TX
214-465-7311

Lazy Eye Ltd.
1521 Folson Street
Eau Claire, WI 54703
713-832-9943

Library Of Congress
National Library Service For The Blind
And Visually Handicapped
1291 Taylor Street NW
Washington, DC 20542

Macula Society
Department of Ophthalmology
University Hospitals
Iowa City, IA 52242

Myopia International Research
Foundation
415 Lexington Avenue
Room 705
New York, NY 10017

National Association Of Optometrists
And Opticians
18903 S. Miles Road
Cleveland, OH 44128

National Association For The Visually
Handicapped
305 E. 24th Street
New York, NY 10010

National Accreditation Council Of
Agencies Serving The Blind And
Visually Handicapped
79 Madison Avenue

National Childrens Eye Care
Foundation
1101 Connecticut Avenue NW
Suite 700
Washington, DC 20036

National Eye Research Foundation
18 S. Michigan Avenue
Chicago, IL 60603

National Eye Institute
Information Office
National Institute of Health
Building 31, Room 6A32
Bethesda, MD 20205

National Institute On Glaucoma Control
1140 Connecticut Avenue NW
Suite 606
Washington, DC 20036
202-466-4555

National Industries For The Blind
1455 Broad Street
Bloomfield, NJ 07003
201-338-3804

National Retinitis Pigmentosa
Foundation
8331 Mindale Circle
Baltimore, MD 21207
301-655-1011

New Eyes For The Needy
P.O. Box 332
Short Hills, NJ 07078
201-376-4903

Orton Dyslexia Society
724 York Road
Baltimore, MD 21204

Recording For The Blind
20 Rozel Road
Princeton, NJ 08540
212-517-9820

Research To Prevent Blindness, Inc.
598 Madison Avenue
New York, NY 10022
212-752-4333

Retina Society
100 Charles River Plaza
Boston, MA 12114

Retinitis Pigmentosa Foundation
1401 Mt. Royal Avenue
4th Floor
Baltimore, MD 21217

Society Of Eye Surgeons
International Eye Foundation
7801 Norfolk Avenue
Bethesda, MD 20814

Veterans Administration
810 Vermont Avenue NW
Washington, DC 20420
202-389-3775

Volunteers For Vision
P.O. Box 2211
Austin, TX 78768

Directory of State Services For The Visually Handicapped*†

AL   Voc. Rehab., 2129 E. South Blvd. POB 11586, Montgomery 36111
AK   Office of Voc. Rehab., Pouch F, Mail Sta. 0581, Juneau 99811
AZ   Rehab. Svcs. Bureau, Dept. Econ. Sec., 1535 West Jefferson, Suite 155, Phoenix 85007
AR   Dept. of Soc. & Rehab. Svcs., 1801 Rebsamen Pk. Rd., POB 3781, Little Rock 72203
CA   Dept. of Rehab., Health & Welf. Agency, 722 Capitol Mall, Sacramento 95814
CO   Div. of Rehab., Dept. Soc. Svcs., 1575 Sherman St., Denver 80203
CT   Bd. of Ed. & Svcs. for Blind, 170 Ridge Rd., Wethersfield 06109
DE   Del. Bureau for Vis. Impaired, Dept. Health and S.S., 305 W. 8th St., Wilmington 19801
DC   Soc. & Rehab. Admin., Dept. Human Res., 122 C St., N.W., 8 Fl., Washington 20001
FL   Bureau Blind Services, Dept. of Ed., 1309 Winewood Blvd., Tallahassee 32301
GA   Dept. Human Res., Div. Voc. Rehab., 47 Trinity Ave., Atlanta 30334
GU   Div. Voc. Rehab., Bd. of Control Voc. Rehab., Dept. of Ed., POB 10-C, Agana 96910
HI   Div. Voc. Rehab., Dept. Soc. Svcs., Queen Liliuokalani Bldg., POB 339, Honolulu 96809
ID   Idaho Comm. for Blind, Statehouse, Boise 83720
IL   Bd. Voc. Ed. & Rehab., Div. Voc. Rehab., 623 E. Adams St., Springfield 62706
IN   Indiana Rehab. Svcs., 1028 Illinois Bldg., 17 W. Market St., Indianapolis 46204
IA   Comm. for the Blind, 4th & Keosauqua, Des Moines 50309
KS   Svcs. for Blind & Vis. Handicapped, Soc. & Rehab. Svce., 2700 W. 6th St., Topeka 66606
KY   Bur. of Rehab. Svcs., Capital Plaza Office Tower, Frankfort 40601
LA   La. Health & Human Res., Family Svce., 755 Riverside N. Box 44065, Baton Rouge70804
ME   Bureau of Rehab., 32 Winthrop St., Augusta 04330
MD   Div. Voc. Rehab., State Dept. Ed., Bx 8717, Balt./Wash. Intnl. Airport, Baltimore 21240
MA   Mass Commission for Blind, 39 Boylston St., Boston 02116
MI   Dept. Soc. Svcs., Div. Svcs. for Blind, 300 S. Capitol Ave., Lansing 48926
MN   State Svcs. for Blind & Vis. Hamdicapped, 1745 University Ave., St. Paul 55104
MS   Vocational Rehab., for Blind, POB 4872, Jackson 39216
MO   Bur. for Blind, Dept. Soc. Svcs., B'way State Office Bldg., Jefferson City 65101
MT   Visual Svce. Div., Dept. Soc. & Rehab. Svcs., POB 1723, Helena 59601
NB   Svce. for the Visually Impaired, 1047 South St., Lincoln 68502
NV   Bureau of Svcs. for Blind, Dept. Human Res., 308 N. Curry St., Rm 200, Carson City89701
NH   State Dept. Ed., Div. Voc. Rehab., 105 Loudon Rd., Bldg 3, Concord 03301
NJ   Comm. for Blind & Vis. Impaired, 1100 Raymond Blvd., Newark 07102
NM   Dept. of Ed., 231 Washington Ave., POB 1830, Santa Fe 87503
NY   State Dept. Soc. Svcs., Comm. for Visually Handicapped, 40 No. Pearl St., Albany 12243
NC   Div. Svcs. for Blind, N.C. Dept. Human Res, 410 N. Boylan Ave., Box 2658, Raleigh 27602
ND   Div. Voc. Rehab., 1025 N. 3rd St., Box 1037, Bismarck 58501
OH   Rehab. Svcs. Comm., 4656 Heaton Rd., Columbus 43229
OK   Dept. of Instit. Rehab. Svcs., Div. Rehab. & Vis. Svcs., POB 25352, Oklahoma City 73125
OR   Comm. for Blind, 535 S.E. 12th Ave., Portland 97214
PA   Dept. Pub Welf, Bur for Vis Handicapped, Capital Assn. Bldg., POB2675 Harrisburg 17120
PR   Asst. Secy. Voc. Rehab., Dept. Soc. Svcs., POB 1118, Hato Rey 00919
RI   Dept. of Soc. & Rehab. Svce., Svcs. for Blind, 46 Aborn St., Providence 02903
SC   Comm. for Blind, POB 11638, Capital Sta., Columbia 29211
SD   Dept. Soc. Svcs., Div. Rehab. Svcs, State Office Bldg., Illinois St., Pierre 57501
TN   Div. Svcs. for the Blind, Dept. Human Svcs., 303 State Office Bldg., Nashville 37219
TX   State Comm. for Blind, POB 12866, Capital Sta., 800 City Natnl Bank Bldg, Austin 78711
UT   Div. 0f Rehab. Svcs., 250 E. 5th Utah St. Bd. of Ed., Salt Lake City 84111
VT   Div. for the Blind & Vis Handicapped, Dept. Soc. & Rehab. Svcs, 81 River St., Montpelier 0560
VA   Virginia Comm. for Visually Handicapped, 3003 Parkwood Ave., Richmond 23221
VI   Dept. Soc. Welf., Div. Voc. Rehab., POB 539, St. Thomas 00801
WA   Off. Svcs. for Blind, Dept. Soc. & Health Svcs., 3411 So Alaska St., Seattle 98118
WV   Div. Voc. Rehab, State Bd. Voc. Ed, State Capital, P&G Bldg, Washington St., Charleston 2530
WS   Div. Voc. Rehab., Dept. Health & Soc. Svcs., 1 W. Wilson St., Rm 720, Madison 53702
WY   Div. Voc. Rehab., Hathaway Bldg., West, Cheyenne 82002

*Compiled by Massachusetts Eye & Ear Infirmary from AFB Directory of agencies serving the visually handicapped.
†Reprinted with permission from the publisher. Copyright © PRD for Ophthalmology 1988 edition. Published my Medical Economics Company, Inc., Oradell, NJ 07649

INDEX

INDEX